D0392171

SHOBUN

SHOGUN

SHOBUN

A Forgotten War Crime in the Pacific

Michael J. Goodwin

edited by Don Graydon

STACKPOLE
BOOKS

Copyright © 1995 by Stackpole Books

Published by
STACKPOLE BOOKS
5067 Ritter Road
Mechanicsburg, PA 17055

All rights reserved, including the right to reproduce this book or portions
thereof in any form or by any means, electronic or mechanical, including photo-
copying, recording, or by any information storage and retrieval system,
without permission in writing from the publisher. All inquiries should be
addressed to Stackpole Books, 5067 Ritter Road, Mechanicsburg, PA 17055.

Printed in the United States of America

ISBN 0-8117-1518-3

*To the eleven young men
who flew off into the night
to do battle with the enemy*

Contents

Foreword

The Second World War lasted six years, cost the lives of forty-six million combatants and civilians, and unhinged and recast the framework of international politics, unleashing forces with which the remaining half of the twentieth century had to deal. The geographic reach of the conflict was unprecedented, as was its ideological and military complexity. For America, belligerency closed an era when the United States served as the arbiter of the balance of power in Europe and Asia and opened a new era in which two superpowers contested global supremacy with ideas and military power. For the U.S. Navy, the 1939–1945 conflict posed the immense challenges of preparing in the twilights of neutrality and then conducting operations on the daunting scale demanded by a two-ocean war.

These great themes hover over and explain this extraordinary account of the last flight of PBY No. 08233 of Patrol Bombing Squadron 29 (VPB-29) off the southeast coast of the Celebes in October 1944 and the fate of her eleven-man crew. Prewar American naval strategists supposed that, in a war between the United States and Japan, the enemy would occupy the Philippines, then an American territory, and the U.S. Fleet would counterattack along the line West Coast–Hawaii–Marianas. Hard upon the attack on Pearl Harbor, however, the Japanese occupied the Dutch

East Indies, most of New Guinea, and the Solomon Islands, thus menacing Australia and New Zealand, British dominions that looked theretofore to the Admiralty in London for protection. Inasmuch as the Royal Navy was at the time tied down blockading Germany, fighting the Battle of the Atlantic, and checking the Italians in the Mediterranean, and because the British front in Malaya and Burma was collapsing, London persuaded Washington to include its southwestern Pacific dominions in the American theaters of strategic responsibility. This forced U.S. Navy planners to recast completely their basic strategy, deploy carrier task forces to the Coral Sea, and inaugurate the American counteroffensive not with a blow in the Central Pacific but, instead, with a movement up the Solomon Islands.

Meanwhile, the U.S. Army's Southwest Pacific command secured the Papuan Peninsula and fought westward along the northern coast of New Guinea. These offensives, shielding Australia, ultimately joined 500 miles south of the Philippines and then converged in October 1944 with the recently opened Central Pacific front. Thus, when PBY No. 08233 took off for the last time on October 1, Gen. Douglas MacArthur's army and Adm. William "Bull" Halsey's fleet were within three weeks of descending on Leyte Gulf to liberate the Filipinos. Constant harassing operations by Navy maritime patrol bomber squadrons like VPB-29 covered the flanks and rearward areas of these great fleet movements, maintained a combat tempo to the campaign during the lulls between major landings and battles, tied down enemy forces by hindering their movements, and contributed immeasurably to the isolation of the vital Dutch East Indies. This severed Japan's connection with her source of oil. Japanese industry froze, thus making less costly the final American approach to the Home Islands.

The story of PBY No. 08233 illustrated other aspects of the U.S. Navy's conduct of the war. The outcome of the expansion of the prewar Navy from fewer than 200,000 sailors to a wartime high of more than 3,000,000 is reflected in the makeup of the patrol bomber's crew. On board for that last flight were, among others, a farmboy from Indiana, a landscaping student from Kentucky, and the well-educated son of Jewish immigrants who settled in St. Paul. None were professional Navy men; only one had entered the service before Pearl Harbor. Yet by late 1944 these and other members of the "citizen navy" manned what was surely the finest, most lethal fleet of the war, a force that dealt smashing blows to its Axis rivals from Guadalcanal to the Greenland Air Gap to the Normandy coast and the Philippine Sea. And in doing so, they transformed the world.

VPB-29, for instance, staged from Perth, Australia, a country so changed by war and the accompanying American influx that its newspapers began to carry Major League baseball scores, and 15,000 Australian girls became American war brides. The links between Melbourne and Washington lasted long after the conflict in which they were born. Soon after World War II, Australia and New Zealand exchanged documents with the United States ratifying the ANZUS Alliance, which changed forever the face of Southwest Pacific politics. And one of those Australian war brides married the father of our author, Michael Goodwin, who grew to manhood in a Cold War shaped, and surely bettered, by the generation that flew, fought, and died for the United States during World War II.

The men flying PBY No. 08233 went down during an attack on an enemy installation, and the cruel end of these naval aviators at the hands of their Japanese captors suggests another truth about the larger conflict. Americans and their British and French allies occasionally committed terrible atrocities against captured prisoners of war. These incidents, however, were remarkably few and always isolated, invariably directed against individuals, commonly the product of white-hot anger, and never condoned by higher command or graced by the sanction of national warmaking policy. On the other hand, the Germans and their Japanese allies made war in a qualitatively different way, since the story of PBY No. 08233 was quite as legal under Tokyo's system as were the crematoriums of Auschwitz under laws enacted by Berlin.

Nonetheless, vengefulness for these wrongs played a surprisingly slight role in America's occupation policy—to the longlasting discomfort of the instant victims and their families. Informed by the sorry consequences of the vengeance of the Treaty of Versailles, the Americans who occupied the countries of their former Axis enemies adopted policies of conciliation and the balm of purposeful forgiving. Taking this approach meant that justice was not always served, the wicked were not always punished, and punishments for war crimes seldom matched the offenses committed.

Our author explains that injustice is always hard to understand on a personal level, but the grand American policy of forgiveness and reconciliation miraculously transformed the bitterest of wartime enemies into the staunchest of Cold War allies and went far in the service of the larger cause of postwar freedom, security, and peace. Such magnanimity surely honored the memory of the men of PBY No. 08233 and made their tragic, ultimate sacrifice all the more worthwhile.

Robert W. Love, Jr.
United States Naval Academy
Annapolis, Maryland

Preface

My father lost his life a few months before I was born. He died in a war that happened a long time ago, a war I could not know. I was aware that he had existed, and that my mother called him a wonderful man, but I did not know much else. My grandfather told me a few stories about him, even a little bit about how he died. He had been shot down in the Pacific in World War II, captured by the Japanese, and later killed by them.

Being young and immature, I did not pay much attention to these stories. I was happy living with my mother, stepfather, half sister, and half brother. In my early adult years I spent my energy raising a family with my wife. My grandparents passed away, and the memory of the man who had fathered me grew further and further from me.

In 1987 my oldest son was accepted into the United States Naval Academy. My father had been a Navy pilot, and I began to think more about Bill Goodwin, this man I had never known. During a visit to the Academy, I had the opportunity to talk to some members of the faculty, and I asked one of the history instructors how I might find out something of my father and his short Naval career. He gave me the name and address of another history instructor, a man who specialized in the Second World War. With that one name and address I began a personal journey of discovery that was to last seven years.

I wrote to history instructor Dr. Robert W. Love, Jr., and his reply started me on my way. Over the next six years I wrote hundreds of letters to individuals who might have information and to organizations, government agencies, and foreign governments. I tracked down former members of the two Navy squadrons my father had flown with. I visited the commanding officer of the squadron he was with when his plane was shot down. In 1989 my family and I attended a reunion of one of those squadrons, and I talked face to face with men who had lived and flown with my father.

I pestered the people at the National Archives in Washington, D.C., until they found the records of the war crimes trials of the Japanese who were involved in my father's execution. After that I spent many hours at the Archives, copying hundreds of pages of documents. The Naval Historical Center in Washington, D.C., provided me with combat diaries and other information on the Navy squadrons involved.

The most difficult job was trying to make contact with more men who had known my father and who might tell what had happened to him. I started this part of my search with a notice I found in the back of an old issue of the Naval Institute's *Proceedings,* advertising a reunion of the last squadron my father had flown with, which led to a mailing list of a few former squadron members. I wrote letters. Of four letters written, one would be returned, unopened; another would receive no response; and of the two letters that brought in replies, only one might contain useful information or a few new names and addresses. And then I would send out more letters.

Every now and then I struck it rich. Someone would reply with five or six pages of details about my father and the other crewmen on the downed plane. Some of my correspondents found old photos from the Pacific war, hidden away for years—a few showing my father.

Month by month the pile of information grew. Slowly, I began to see a clearer picture of the man I never knew. I learned not only about my father, but also about the ten men who died with him. To me, these men were no longer just names on paper, but real people with families.

I learned that I was the sole offspring of any of the eleven men on the plane; my father was the only one who had married. I successfully contacted five families of the ten men who flew with my father on his final mission.

The story of those men became my obsession, and as a catharsis, I began this book. These men and their fate should not be forgotten.

Acknowledgments

More than a hundred individuals helped me in my efforts to research and write this book. Without their assistance and understanding, my father and his comrades would still be to me just a handful of names from the distant past.

I owe a great deal to the former members of Navy patrol squadrons VP-33 and VP-101. Special gratitude goes to John Zubler, George Favorite, Bob Gates, Gardner Burt, Don Johnson, and Bob Hendrie of VP-33; and to George Castille, L. E. "Steve" Johnson, Joe Gardner, George Smith, and his late brother Bud Smith from VP-101. To help tell this story, these men opened their scrapbooks and photo albums, their hearts and memories.

To learn more about the personal side of my father, I wrote to and visited his childhood friends. Tommy Ruggiero, Henry Bastoni, and Alfred Pizzoti (who has since passed away) shared with me their memories of their dear pal.

I located family members of the following men who flew with my father: Nilva, Zollinger, Schilling, Cart, Kuhlman, and Harbecke. These families went out of their way to provide stories, personal letters, and photos.

The historical details of this book came from the voluminous war records of the National Archives, Washington, D.C.; the United

States Naval Historical Center, Washington Navy Yard; the Military Personnel Records Center, St. Louis; and, most importantly, from Dr. H. Muslimin Su'ud of Kendari, Indonesia, and Michiel Hegener of the Netherlands. From their field work in Sulawesi (formerly Celebes), Indonesia, Dr. Su'ud and Mr. Hegener were able to provide names and facts not known to any American source.

Finally, much credit must go to my wife, Nancy, who put up with me during the years I spent poring over piles of books, letters, and documents and pounding away on my keyboard. Her support and understanding is much appreciated.

Prologue

On October 1, 1944, the airmen aboard PBY No. 08233, a Navy patrol bomber, flew against a Japanese foe that had its back to the wall. The eleven U.S. fliers who took the night-raiding seaplane into the western Pacific skies that evening knew the Japanese reputation for ferocity—a ferocity sharpened by humiliating reversals in the war. And they knew the horror stories about captured airmen beheaded in a gruesome World War II version of the samurai code of Bushido.

During the first six months of the war, Japan won victory after victory. But starting with the Battle of Midway, the fortunes of war changed dramatically for the armed forces of the Empire of Japan. By September 1944, when the U.S. Navy set up PBY operations on the Dutch East Indies island of Morotai, American forces had advanced all across the Pacific. The Japanese had been pushed from the Solomon Islands, New Guinea, the Gilbert Islands, and the Marshall Islands. The home islands of Japan were coming under attack by American carrier raids, and B-29 bombers had started hitting Japan from bases in China.

By the time PBY No. 08233 took to the air on its final mission, the Japanese in the Celebes Islands were beginning to feel cut off from the rest of the war. With the Allied invasion of Morotai, their

Celebes bases came within range of large formations of land-based aircraft. Along with Borneo and the southern Philippines, the Celebes became a major target of the U.S. 13th Army Air Force. The Air Force went after Japanese shipping by day while the PBY flying boats—the "Black Cats"—pounded the Japanese at night. Anything that moved was shot or bombed.

By late 1944, Admiral Tamotsu Furukawa, commander of Japan's 23rd Naval Air Flotilla at Kendari in the Celebes, had few combat aircraft left to command. Nearly all had fallen victim to Allied air raids and to the demand for combat aircraft for the battles raging across the Pacific, and the frustrated Japanese were not able to do much about it. Even the troops manning the antiaircraft batteries, who at least had a chance to shoot back, were being hit hard by fighters and bombers.

The outcome of the war was looking bleak for Japan, and the Japanese at Kendari could see why. With almost all their aircraft gone and most of their motorboats sunk, the Japanese could not send or receive supplies, and troop movement was next to impossible. Bombing raids were becoming heavier and more regular. And they could do little but sit there and take it.

For a nation of warriors who prided themselves on their fighting spirit, the inability to get to the enemy was taking its toll. Their morale was slipping fast. They hungered for an opportunity to retaliate against the increasingly victorious Allies. For the Japanese occupiers of Kendari, the October 1 flight of PBY No. 08233 was about to provide that opportunity.

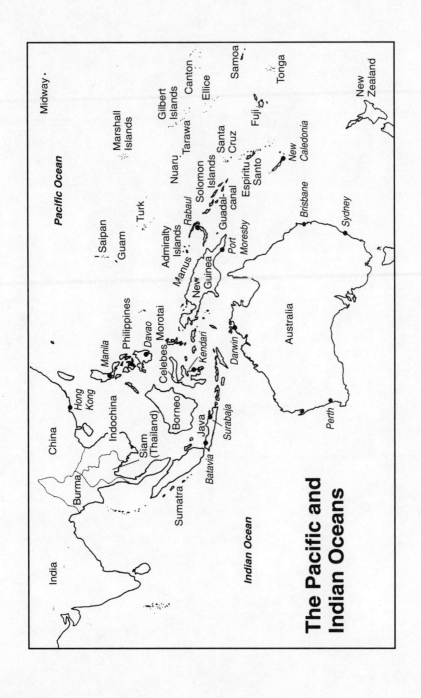

The Pacific and Indian Oceans

Chapter 1

The Black Cats

The U.S. Navy seaplane tender USS *Tangier* lay swinging at anchor just offshore from the small southwest Pacific island of Morotai. As the sun started to sink into the tropical western horizon on the evening of October 1, 1944, a plane crew left the *Tangier* and transferred to PBY No. 08233 in one of the ship's motorboats.

The eleven airmen had more on their minds than the upcoming night raid against the Japanese. Rumor had it that their squadron was about to rotate back to the United States. Some of the men had been in the Pacific for three years, and they were all eager to return home, as evidenced by recent letters to friends and family.

Gen. Douglas MacArthur's forces had invaded Morotai two weeks earlier, and sporadic fighting was still taking place on this island in the Moluccas, some 300 miles southeast of the Philippines. Within days of the Allied landings on Morotai, the *Tangier* and three other seaplane tenders had steamed in and dropped anchor. Moored around the four tenders were their charges, the Navy's big PBY Catalina flying boats.

As soon as the eleven men boarded their plane that evening, they started the preflight check. The PBY soon slipped its mooring and started the takeoff run from Morotai's sheltered waters. The run took longer than usual. Besides her full combat load of fuel, bombs, and ammunition, and her regular air crew of nine, she carried the weight of two extra crewmen. A few minutes after 5:00 P.M. the heavily laden plane broke the ocean's grip and lifted into the air. She was under way on a "Black Cat" night patrol over enemy waters, looking for Japanese shipping to sink.

The plane was a PBY-5 model, a true flying boat that could take off and land only on water. She was powered by two tough and reliable Pratt & Whitney 1200-horsepower R-1830-82 radial engines—basically the same engine that ran the B-17, B-24, B-25, C-47, and many other aircraft in America's arsenal.

The PBY name derives from its mission, Patrol Bomber, and from the code letter, Y, for its manufacturer, Consolidated Aircraft. For a combat aircraft, the PBY was relatively well equipped for her crew's comfort. She provided two sleeping bunks in a separate compartment, a hot plate for coffee and food, and even a toilet of sorts.

The PBY Catalina was both beautiful and ugly at the same time. She had a huge 104-foot-long wing that sat high on a pylon above the fuselage. Her nose was stubby; the single tail rudder was rather large and stood high above the rest of the plane. A Plexiglas blister on each side just behind the wing housed heavy machine guns. The 64-foot-long fuselage was shaped like a boat's hull, and the tip of each wing was actually a float that folded down when the plane took off or landed on water.

By the time the United States entered World War II in December 1941, the PBY was almost seven years old and considered obsolete by many in the Navy. Flying with only two engines made the plane, with a gross weight of 32,000 pounds, much slower than the big four-engine aircraft, such as the B-17 or B-24. Her top cruising speed was about 110 miles an hour, with a maximum of about 195 miles an hour for a brand-new plane on a good day. The PBY's slow speed and large size made her an easy target for enemy fighters and antiaircraft fire, a tragic fact her crews learned early in the war.

Her main redeeming qualities were her long range and rugged construction. She used far less fuel than four-engine planes, giving her the extended range she became known for. The PBY could stay in the air for well over twenty hours and could cover 2,500 miles. She could also take a great deal of punishment and still get her crew home.

The PBY flew its missions with one .50 caliber machine gun in each of the two Plexiglas blisters and a .30 caliber machine gun in the nose. Another .30 caliber could be stuck out the rear hatch under the tail once she became airborne. Because the hull had to be watertight, her load of bombs, depth charges, and torpedoes was hung under the big wings instead of in a bomb bay.

Within the first few weeks of the war, Allied forces in the South Pacific lost most of their combat aircraft to the better-trained and better-equipped Japanese air forces. Only two squadrons of American PBYs were deployed in the South Pacific when the war began. These squadrons stationed in the Philippines flew an earlier model, the PBY-4, with slightly smaller engines than the PBY-5 and sliding hatches instead of the Plexiglas blisters.

These PBYs were quickly pressed into service searching for the advancing Japanese forces, bombing Japanese invasion fleets, and flying personnel out of the war zone. Hundreds of military and civilian personnel flew to safety in Australia aboard PBYs as the Allied resistance collapsed in the Philippines and the Dutch East Indies in early 1942. When the PBYs located advancing Japanese forces, they sometimes ended up being the only planes available to carry out an attack. These bombing attacks usually proved unsuccessful, and losses mounted rapidly.

Those who thought the PBY obsolete were almost proven right. The Japanese easily shot down many PBYs on patrol and destroyed many others on bombing and strafing runs that targeted PBY bases or moorings. It was not always one-sided, however: Catalina machine gunners successfully shot down a number of the attacking Japanese fighters. The two squadrons lost forty-two Catalinas to the Japanese before withdrawing from combat. During this fighting, additional PBYs were flown in from Hawaii, and a few were picked up from the Dutch forces as the Dutch were pushed out of the East Indies. Almost all these planes were lost.

In March 1942, the remnants of the two squadrons ended up in Perth, Western Australia, with only three serviceable aircraft left. The squadrons were consolidated into one, VP-101. The men stayed in Perth for many months, recuperating, rebuilding, and retraining.

The PBY Catalina flew and fought from those terrible first days right up to the end of the war. The Battle of Midway in June 1942 was the first major battle since America's earlier defeats in the Pacific in which PBYs played a significant role. The Japanese Naval High Command had hoped to destroy what remained of the American fleet after the attack on Pearl Harbor, but American Naval Intelligence broke the Japanese Navy's signaling code, giving U.S. forces warning of the coming battle. On June 3 a PBY Catalina spotted the first of the enemy ships some 700 miles out, approaching Midway. The sighting started the battle that turned the tide for the United States in the Pacific war. Other Catalinas from Midway joined in by attacking the Japanese with torpedoes that night, severely damaging a transport ship.

The next major battle, on August 7, 1942, was for the island of Guadalcanal in the Solomon Islands, where the Japanese were building a strategically critical airfield. During the early phases of the Battle of Guadalcanal, American forces were desperately short of combat aircraft. A few old PBYs, pressed into service as daylight bombers and torpedo planes, had only limited success.

Squadrons of PBYs moved up to the Solomon Islands area and operated from seaplane tenders anchored nearby. The tenders gave the Catalinas their operating flexibility, since the PBYs needed only a large bay or sheltered cove from which to land and take off, plus the tenders to service the planes and to feed and house their crews. When combat operations moved, the PBY squadrons could quickly hop to the next base and make use of a different tender.

The PBY patrol squadrons began to change their combat role and work out new tactics during the Battle of Guadalcanal. Inferior in combat because of slow speed and poor maneuverability, the PBYs were relegated to use in antisubmarine patrols, administrative flights, and search-and-rescue missions. But there was one air combat role the Navy quickly learned the PBY could perform well: nighttime attacks against enemy shipping.

PBY crews first proved the effectiveness of night attacks during the early stages of the Battle of Midway. The crews flew long patrols over enemy waters at night and dropped delayed-action bombs from an altitude of a hundred feet or less. After spotting an enemy ship, they would cut back on engine power and quietly glide down to drop their bomb load on the unsuspecting target. Delayed-action fuses enabled the planes to get away before the bombs exploded. The PBYs could attack and escape before the enemy even knew they were there.

The PBYs sank more than 700,000 tons of Japanese shipping this way. The plane was modified slightly to aid the newly developed night tactics. The famed Norden bomb sight, useless at low altitudes, was removed from the nose and replaced with a radio altimeter for help in flying close to the water. The PBYs were repainted flat black to hide them from enemy lookouts. As a result of the repainting, the Catalinas earned a new name: For the rest of the war they would be called the "Black Cats."

A Black Cat crew regularly consisted of three commissioned pilots and six enlisted men. The pilots rotated flying during the long night missions, with two at the controls and one navigating.

These nighttime PBY missions could be extremely successful. On the night of September 23, 1944, Lt. (jg) William Sumpter spotted a Japanese seaplane tender refueling two destroyer escorts. Sumpter dropped a string of four 500-pound bombs, sinking all three ships with a single bombing run.

The Black Cat squadrons were assigned many concurrent roles. Some PBYs flew Black Cat night-attack missions while others flew antisubmarine patrols or rescue missions. The logbooks of many pilots show that their flights jumped between different types of missions. During the war there were never more than about twenty PBY Black Cat squadrons operating in the Pacific, with twelve to fifteen planes each. But their contribution to the war effort was far greater than their numbers would indicate.

The PBY was responsible for sinking more enemy shipping than any other single type of aircraft. At the same time that these ships were being sent to the bottom, thousands of Allied airmen, soldiers, and sailors were saved from the ocean or from capture by the Japanese through the daring action of PBY crews. It can be said that the PBY was the only combat aircraft to save more lives than it took.

Chapter 2

The Americans

The PBY Black Cat that took to the air from the waters off Morotai the evening of October 1, 1944, was commanded by Lt. John "Jack" Schenck of the U.S. Naval Reserve. After getting his plane in the air and flying straight and level, Schenck pointed its nose to the southwest and flew out over the Molucca Sea toward the Celebes Islands. Schenck's assigned patrol area was the southeast coast of the Celebes, specifically the waters around the coastal town of Kendari. The excellent harbor and nearby airfield occupied by the Japanese made it a major strategic military location.

The Celebes Islands at that time were part of the colonial Dutch East Indies. Today the main island is called Sulawesi and is one of the larger of the thousands of islands that make up the nation of Indonesia. It lies some five hundred miles south of the Philippines, between the land masses of Borneo and New Guinea. Some say the odd-shaped island with its four long fingers of land has the form of a spider; others say it looks like an orchid.

Kendari was (and still is) a small mining town. It had been the local Dutch administrative and military center for the southeast Celebes before the Japanese invaded the Dutch East Indies. Even today Kendari is the Indonesian governmental administrative center for the same area. Sometime before the Second World War began in the Pacific, the Dutch built a small army base within the town and a military airfield a few miles away.

Not much more than a month after Japan's December 7, 1941, attack on Pearl Harbor, the Japanese invaded Kendari. The highly trained and well-equipped Japanese quickly overran the small mixed force of Dutch and Indonesian soldiers. They took over the airfield and expanded it into a large base that became the home of the Imperial Japanese Navy's 23rd Air Flotilla. The airfield was used as a rest and training base for Japanese Naval Air Forces and as a staging area for raids on Allied forces and bases as far south as Australia's northern coast. Because of its harbor, Kendari became the chief Japanese occupation administration center and supply base for the southeast Celebes and Japanese forces farther south.

The Japanese easily conquered all of the Dutch East Indies. The Imperial Japanese Army and the Imperial Japanese Navy split the responsibility for administering these conquered islands, and the Celebes fell under the Navy's control. Kendari ended up with a garrison of about 1,500 Japanese naval troops, not including those at the nearby airfield.

Capt. Gosuke Taniguchi of the Imperial Japanese Navy took command of the garrison in mid-September 1944. Japanese troops were quartered all around town, with headquarters staff in the old Dutch Army base buildings close to the shore of Kendari Bay. Besides the usual barracks, kitchen, mess hall, offices, and maintenance buildings, the Dutch had also built a stockade that the Japanese turned into a small detention center and prison.

Lt. (jg) William Francis "Bill" Goodwin, Jr., second in command of the fated PBY Black Cat No. 08233, was born on March 11, 1920, in Plymouth, Massachusetts. At that time, Plymouth was a typical small New England town of about 10,000 people. Goodwin's father, the town's postmaster, was the son of John Goodwin, who had been born in 1863 on a ship full of Irish immigrants on their way to America.

Bill Goodwin, Sr., was born on a farm in Hinsdale, Massachusetts, in 1890. He was a self-educated man, having quit school in the

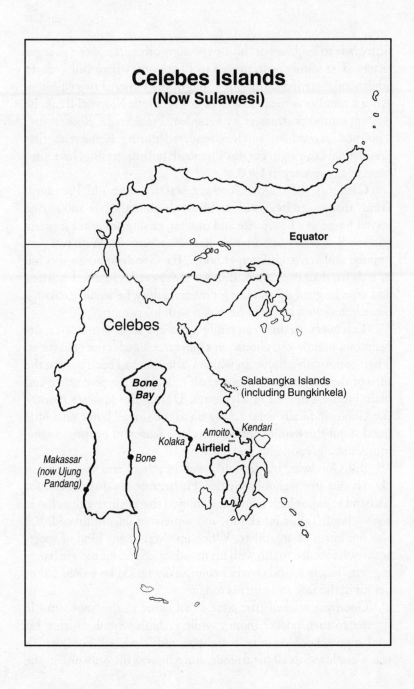

Celebes Islands
(Now Sulawesi)

Equator

Celebes

Bone
Bay

Salabangka Islands
(including Bungkinkela)

Kolaka

Amoito

Kendari

Airfield

Bone

Makassar
(now Ujung
Pandang)

fifth grade to help support his two younger brothers and five younger
sisters. The family soon moved to Plymouth, where Bill grew to
adulthood, married Catherine Clough, and fathered two children.
After a number of years as a clerk at Plymouth National Bank, he
was appointed postmaster by President Franklin D. Roosevelt—
a political reward for services rendered during Roosevelt's first
presidential campaign. He was Plymouth postmaster until his retire-
ment at age seventy in 1960.

Catherine (Clough) Goodwin was from an old Plymouth
family that traced its American history back to the late 1600s. She
stayed home as a housewife and mother, raising daughter Jeanette
and son Bill, who was born two years after his sister. With two very
popular and active children at home, the Goodwin house was full
of kids from all over town. Bill was always very close to his sister,
and after he grew up and left for overseas duty, he would exchange
more letters with her than he would with his parents.

This average American family lived in a large two-story, four-
bedroom, middle-class house on a quiet tree-lined residential street.
Their comfortable home, in which Catherine had been born at the
turn of the century, was about a half mile from the post office and
main business district of Plymouth. During the summer months
the Goodwin family would move up to their small home on a little
pond about three miles out of town for a season of boating, swim-
ming, fishing, cookouts, and parties.

Bill Goodwin, Jr., did fairly well in school and was active in
church and after-school activities. He became the drum major for
his band in junior high school and enjoyed singing in the glee club in
high school. Tall, a bit skinny, and somewhat uncoordinated, Bill
was not much of an athlete. When involved in any kind of sports
activity, he tended to run with his mouth open and his tongue hang-
ing out. Teachers and coaches continually feared he would fall or
get hit in the face and bite his tongue.

Goodwin worked part time as an usher in the town's movie
theater to earn pocket money while in high school. During his
later high school years he bought an old Model-A Ford, which
was a big hit with all his friends, since he was the only one in the

bunch who owned one. After high school graduation ceremonies, the gang piled into the old Ford and drove up to Boston for a big night on the town.

From the time he entered third grade, Goodwin wanted to become a pilot. He collected books and magazines on flying and the aircraft of the day. Among his most prized possessions was his collection of the airplane trading cards that came in packs of Wings cigarettes as a promotional gimmick. He built wooden model airplanes and even a small model airport. He enthusiastically participated in his high school's Flying Club. And in his senior yearbook he listed his hobby as aviation and wrote that he wanted to "Fly from Pole to Pole."

During his boyhood summers Goodwin would hike out to the small grass airfield not far from his parents' summer home to watch planes take off and land. As he watched, he told himself that someday he would be a pilot. Any time he traveled, he made a point of visiting the local airport to watch the planes and take pictures of them for his scrapbooks.

Bill Goodwin, Jr., graduated from Plymouth High School in June 1939. He was six feet tall and very slender. With his blue eyes and brown hair, he had no trouble attracting girls and spent a good deal of his time pursuing them. After graduation he moved to Providence, Rhode Island, to work and earn money for college. The following year he was accepted at American International College in Springfield, Massachusetts. During his college summers at home he worked making rope at the Plymouth Cordage plant. His pay envelopes show him earning the grand sum of fifty-four cents per hour, with a few cents going toward the then-new Social Security tax.

While attending college he started to date a young Springfield girl named Ginny Fleming. It was not long before he took her home to Plymouth to meet his parents, and she quickly became a regular visitor at the Goodwin household. By the time Bill went overseas for military duty, he and Ginny were engaged to be married. Even with her fiancée at war, Ginny still occasionally made the trip to Plymouth to visit his parents.

Shortly before America entered World War II, Goodwin tried to fulfill his dream of becoming a pilot by applying for acceptance as a cadet in the U.S. Army Air Corps. He was turned down because of a medical history of fainting as a young child. He had long since outgrown this problem, but the Army was very particular before the country went to war.

When the war started for the United States, the need for military pilots increased dramatically. Old minor medical problems could be overlooked. After two years of college, Goodwin again applied for military flight training, this time with the U.S. Navy. On June 26, 1942, he was accepted as a Naval Aviation Cadet and reported for duty a few weeks later. His military indoctrination and preflight school took place at the University of North Carolina at Chapel Hill. (One of the other young cadets from New England who went through Chapel Hill with Goodwin's group would become famous many years later. He was George Herbert Walker Bush, the forty-first president of the United States.)

After preflight training he shipped off to preliminary flight school just south of Boston at the newly established Naval Air Station in Squantum, not far from Plymouth. Training was demanding, with the students flying six days a week and as many as four training flights per day. With the need for pilots so desperate, they even trained right through Christmas Day of 1942. Squantum was close enough to the houses of some of Goodwin's relatives that he would buzz them in his biplane trainer while on solo flights. His younger cousins would rush out and wave to him as he flew over, wagging his wings at them.

As this preliminary pilot training ended in January 1943, Naval Aviation Cadet Goodwin received a few days' leave. He spent the time at home with his family and friends. Then he waved goodbye to his family and his fiancée, Ginny, as he boarded a train bound for the Navy's huge air training facility in Pensacola, Florida. At Pensacola he got his first taste of flying the Navy's patrol planes. He learned to pilot the PBY-3 and PBY-4, early models of the flying boats he would later handle in the Pacific. After many more grueling days of classroom and flight training, he finally achieved his goal of becoming a pilot. William F. Goodwin, Jr., received his "Wings of Gold" and was commissioned an ensign in the U.S. Naval Reserve on May 28, 1943.

New orders in hand, Goodwin traveled by train to San Diego and then up to Seattle, where he reported to the Seattle Naval Air Station for additional flight training in PBYs and other aircraft. He wrote to his parents from Seattle, telling them that he loved the area and thought it looked much like New England. After completing training at Seattle, he received orders for flight duty in the Pacific. Another train ride took him to San Francisco. From there on August 7, 1943, he boarded the steamship SS *Tyler* for the voyage to Hawaii.

As Bill Goodwin steamed toward Hawaii, the first elements of the PBY patrol squadron he was ordered to join also started their long trip from the United States to the South Pacific. Small groups of PBY patrol planes from squadron VP-33 left North Island Naval Air Station in San Diego and flew to Kaneohe Naval Air Station on Oahu. Ensign Bill Goodwin arrived in Honolulu on August 15, 1943, and two days later reported in at Kaneohe for duty with VP-33.

The green pilot was assigned to a PBY flight crew commanded by Lt. Bob Gates. Ensign George Favorite was the second pilot on the crew, and thus second in command. Goodwin, the least experienced, was the third pilot. Gates and his crew soon started flying patrols and training missions out of Kaneohe. One of the PBY-5s they used for these patrols—the only known PBY-5 model still in existence—is now on permanent display at the National Museum of Naval Aviation in Pensacola, Florida.

A few weeks after arriving in Hawaii, the squadron received orders to pack up and fly west across the Pacific to Perth, Western Australia, where they were to join Fleet Air Wing 10. The PBYs used small, little-known islands as stopping points on the long trip southwestward.

Halfway through its journey, the squadron stopped to assist with the U.S. Marine invasion of the island of Tarawa. For about a week before the battle, the squadron patrolled the seas around Tarawa in a search for Japanese vessels. As soon as the Marines invaded Tarawa, squadron VP-33 continued its island-hopping trip toward Australia. The crews spent several days at each small island, resting, maintaining the PBYs, and flying patrols.

On October 28, 1943, a month and a half after leaving Hawaii, the squadron's planes reached Brisbane, on the east coast of Australia. After two more days and another twenty hours of actual flying, they landed on the Swan River by Perth, some eight thousand miles from Hawaii. Goodwin and his mates quickly settled into their new home. They spent the next few months flying antisubmarine patrols and training missions along the west coast of Australia.

The Americans enjoyed a pleasant life while stationed in Perth. Officers of the PBY squadrons stayed in comfortable buildings at the University of Western Australia. Compared to their Australian counterparts American servicemen seemed wealthy, as the local women quickly realized. Even though it was against regulations, American servicemen could obtain certain foods, cigarettes, liquor, and other items that the Australians could not get because of wartime rationing.

Goodwin and another pilot from the squadron, Fred Warbois, bought a small car despite the gasoline shortage. They drained high-powered aviation fuel from their patrol planes to power the car. The 100-plus octane gas caused problems with the little car's engine, but it ran. By the time the men left Perth, their car needed a complete engine overhaul.

Another squadron joined VP-33 in Perth in December. Squadron VP-101 had been engaged in its second combat tour against the Japanese and now was sent to Perth for rest, refitting, and training of replacement personnel. Many of the experienced but war-weary pilots of VP-101 were rotated home, and new pilots were needed. VP-33 had many young pilots, and ten of them were to be transferred to VP-101 in January. Goodwin requested to be one of the ten. He knew VP-33 would soon be moving out to the war zone in New Guinea, and he wanted to stay a little longer to be near a young girl he had met in the city. The transfer was granted. Goodwin remained in Perth when his former squadron left for combat duty in February.

The crew commanded by Lt. Jack Schenck began flying together in the latter part of June 1944, about the time squadron VP-101 shifted operations from Perth to the war zone. Schenck's regular crew consisted of himself, two other commissioned pilots, and six enlisted crewmen.

Jack Schenck was continuing a family tradition of Naval aviation. His father, William, had been a Navy pilot during World War I. Called back to active duty during this new war, William Schenck was serving overseas when his son piloted the mission to Kendari. William and Helen Schenck, of Narberth, Pennsylvania, had only one other child, a daughter a couple of years younger than Jack. Schenck was born on March 26, 1920, which meant that he was two weeks younger than Bill Goodwin.

With the exception of his most senior enlisted crewman, Jack Schenck had been out in the Pacific longer then anyone else in his regular crew. He had left the United States for combat duty in the Pacific during December 1942 and had started flying with VP-101 as a PBY pilot when the squadron left for its second combat tour in the Solomon Islands. He held the position of patrol plane second pilot, which was third in the chain of command. But by the time the squadron was ready to engage in its third and final combat tour, he had been promoted to lieutenant (junior grade) and was commanding his own plane. He was promoted again, to full lieutenant, shortly before the squadron moved to Morotai.

Bill Goodwin had earned promotion to lieutenant (junior grade) and became second in command, and by the time of the October 1 mission to Kendari, Ensign Arthur W. Kuhlman had become the third pilot.

Arthur Kuhlman was the only brother to two older sisters. He was born April 29, 1923, to Arthur H. and Bessie Kuhlman in Inglewood, California. After graduating from Inglewood High School in 1940, he went to work for North American Aviation in its

Southern California plant. Kuhlman became a Naval aviation cadet one year after Japan's attack on Pearl Harbor. He took basic flight training at Hutchinson, Kansas, and then traveled to Corpus Christi, Texas, for advanced training on the flying boats he would pilot in the Pacific. In December 1943 Kuhlman received his commission and wings as a Naval aviator.

In addition to Schenck, Goodwin, and Kuhlman, six enlisted men constituted the regular plane crew. The senior enlisted man, called the plane captain, was equivalent to the Army Air Corps' crew chief on big bombers, and he led the other five. In Schenck's crew, Aviation Machinist Mate 1st Class Harvey Harbecke held that position. From his engineering chair in the pylon, or "the tower," that connected the plane's high wing to its fuselage, the plane captain monitored and controlled the fuel, oil, oil pressure, engine temperature, and other mechanical aspects of the PBY. A small window on each side of his seat allowed him to keep an eye on the engines. Harbecke spoke with the pilots over the plane's intercom system.

Harvey Harbecke was the only regular member of the crew who was in the Navy when the war broke out in the Pacific. This country boy from the rural Southwest had joined the Navy in the middle of 1941, leaving behind his widowed mother, four brothers, and three sisters in the small town of Fowler, Colorado. Because he was just seventeen when he enlisted, his mother had to sign the papers allowing him to join. On the day Pearl Harbor was attacked, Harbecke shipped out from California for his first Pacific duty station. He ended up with VP-101 in Perth while the squadron was rebuilding after being devastated in the early months of the war.

The other enlisted members of Schenck's regular crew were Aviation Radioman 1st Class Joseph Sommer, Aviation Radioman 3rd Class Edwin McMaster, Aviation Machinist Mate 2nd Class Jake Nilva, Aviation Machinist Mate 3rd Class Raymond L. Cart, and Aviation Ordnanceman 1st Class Paul Schilling. Sommer and McMaster were the plane's radio operators: One handled the radio, and the other worked the radar used to spot enemy shipping. Nilva and Cart sat in the two side blisters as lookouts and manned the .50 caliber machine guns. Schilling, the crew's ordnance expert, was stationed on the .30 caliber machine gun in the nose of the plane. (A pharmacist mate—a medic—flew on PBY rescue missions, but he was not part of the regular crew.)

Joe Sommer, an orphan, had no immediate family other than the aunt who had raised him. He may have had a brother who was also in the Navy, though this could not be confirmed. His brother's name may have been either Francis August Sommer or August Francis Sommer. Joe Sommer was a handsome sailor and a good radioman.

Edwin McMaster was the son of James and Clarice McMaster of Chicago. His sister, Miriam, was ten years his junior. McMaster was sworn into the Navy on February 6, 1943. After boot camp and radio school, he shipped out for the Pacific Theater in March 1944 to join VP-101 in Perth. He was nineteen when he started flying with Schenck's crew.

Paul Schilling, a lanky six foot two, was the tallest member of the crew. The youngest of the three sons and one daughter of Jacob and Laura Schilling, Paul was born August 2, 1925, in Clinton, New York. He enlisted in the Navy in September 1942, went to boot camp in Newport, Rhode Island, and attended Aviation Ordnance School in Memphis, Tennessee. After a short leave spent at home, Schilling traveled overseas in March 1943 and eventually joined VP-101 while it was in Australia.

Raymond L. Cart, five foot seven and 120 pounds, was the smallest member of the PBY crew. On their farm in southern Indiana Ralph and Clara Cart raised six boys and two girls. Ray was born January 3, 1925, joined the Navy in March 1943, and was shipped straight out to Perth and VP-101 after initial training and a short leave. He ended up in Schenck's crew in March 1944.

Before leaving for overseas duty, Cart worked out a code with his parents so that they would know where he was stationed. To slip this information past military censors, Cart used a different middle initial between his father's first and last names in the address on each letter he sent home. After several letters his family learned that he was in Perth, but they still did not know why he was there.

Jake Nilva had a more unusual background that the others. He was born on August 10, 1913, in St. Paul, Minnesota, to Jewish

Russian immigrants Louis and Sara Nilva. Jake was the third of five children, three boys and two girls, and the first to be born in America. Like his older brother Allen, Jake was over the draft-age limit of twenty-eight when the war started. He could easily have avoided the war as a civilian. After eleven years of hard work, Jake rose to the position of secretary-treasurer with the Utility Finance Company in St. Paul. He had established himself in the business community and was living very comfortably by the time the Japanese attacked Pearl Harbor. While advancing in the business world, he went to night school, earning college credits and working toward a degree.

Jake had had enough college and business experience to apply for and probably receive a commission as an officer in any of the armed services. With his work experience he could have gone through the entire war in some administrative post far from the front lines. But he would not have it this way. In February 1942 he enlisted in the Navy as a regular sailor so that he could fight for his country. Before doing so he told his family, "I do not want anyone to say that a Jew is taking the easy way out. America is a wonderful country to live in and, if need be, die for."

Nilva took boot camp at the Great Lakes Naval Base, went to Aviation Machinist Mate School in Oklahoma, and completed Naval Air Gunners School in May 1943. He shipped out to the Pacific around the end of June. At the beginning of January 1944 he began flying with VP-101 in Perth, and in May he joined Schenck's crew. Jake was considered the "old man" of the group, and all the others respected him. He was the only one of them who had made a living in the "real world." He was also one of the more experienced crewmen on Schenck's plane, with more than one hundred missions under his belt.

Jake's older brother, Allen, also decided to serve his country in its time of need, and he received a commission in the Army. An attorney in civilian life, he served most of the war in legal staff positions in the India-Burma Theater. Sammy, youngest of the three Nilva brothers, enlisted in the Army Air Corps and eventually worked for the Office of Strategic Services, the predecessor of today's Central Intelligence Agency.

The two extra men who went along on Schenck's October 1 mission were Aviation Machinist Mate 1st Class Walter G. Price and Aviation Radioman 2nd Class Henry T. Zollinger.

Walt Price is something of a mystery. All that is known about him and his family is that his father, Roy L. Price, had a post office box in Pampa, Texas, and that the Price family may have originally come from Louisiana. Walt Price was tall and thin, with a face that looked as if it had been on the losing end of a number of fistfights. He was missing a few teeth. Price had been in the Navy for about as long as his good friend Harvey Harbecke.

Henry Zollinger, called "Hientz" by his family, was the second son of Theodore and Margaret Zollinger. He and his twin sister, Martha, were born December 4, 1921. The family ran a large, successful nursery and landscaping business in Louisville, Kentucky, where Hientz worked for a year between high school and college. The war interrupted his college studies in landscape architecture, and he enlisted in the Navy in July 1942. After boot camp and radio school, Zollinger became a radioman in VP-101.

It must have been crowded in that PBY on the night of the Kendari mission, with eleven men aboard. Though large, the PBY is not designed to carry extra people in comfort. Why two extra men were along may never be known. They did not have to be on board, since the regular crew was complete. None of the former members of the squadron can remember exactly why Price and Zollinger flew with Schenck's men that night.

Possible explanations abound. Other squadron members commonly tagged along on patrol flights in order to log additional flight hours. Walt Price had been a plane captain in a PBY crew that just broke up because its commander had experienced a nervous breakdown from combat fatigue. Price may have wanted to continue logging flight hours while he was temporarily without a regular crew. He was a close friend of Harvey Harbecke; they even double-dated together in Australia. Price may have gone on the mission just to be with his buddy.

Either Price or Zollinger might have been aboard to familiarize himself with Schenck and his crew so that he could replace one of the regulars. Price may have been an extra lookout and gunner on this flight. Zollinger may have helped with one of the radiomen's jobs. Or the two might have simply gone along for the ride.

Some of the men in the plane crew had girlfriends, either back in the States or in Australia. A few of these relationships were serious, but the most serious romance was that of Bill Goodwin and Valerie Storey, a young Australian girl he had met in Perth. One day toward the end of 1943, Goodwin was wandering through Perth and soon became hopelessly lost. When he stopped at a house to ask directions, a pretty teenage girl answered the door. The good-looking young American Naval officer started a conversation, and learned that Valerie was the older of two daughters of an Australian Army captain serving in the Perth area. One thing led to another, and Goodwin started dating this girl while continuing to write to his fianceé, Ginny, at home.

At one point during this whirlwind romance, the entire squadron was restricted to the base as punishment for something its members had done. (The restriction was more than likely the result of one of the wild parties for which squadron VP-33 was famous. A receipt for the cost of one such party at a Perth nightclub shows that much of the charge was for broken glassware and furniture.) As the squadron endured its punishment, a chief warrant officer by the name of George Young came to Goodwin's rescue. Young, a crusty old Navy chief, had fought during the First World War and retired after many years of service. He was called back to active duty for the new war, made a warrant officer, and assigned to VP-33. Young had taken all the young ensigns under his wing, so of course he knew of Goodwin's romance. Young arranged for Goodwin to leave the base and go into town on "official Navy business." Everyone in the squadron, except the commanding officer, knew that Goodwin really was going to visit his Australian sweetheart.

About a month after meeting her, Goodwin started to write about the new girl in his life to his parents and sister. The first mention of Valerie was in a January 24, 1944, letter to Jeanette. Near the bottom of the letter he casually mentioned: "By the way

Nan, I have hitched up to one of these gals over here for my stay because I just have to have some fun. Ginny wrote and told me she was going out with this fellow from work so I don't feel so bad." By April, Goodwin decided to break off his relationship with his fiancée and wrote her a long letter. He was now in love with a different girl. He never heard from Ginny again.

Arthur Kuhlman had a girl waiting for him in Florida. After he received his commission and wings, he was temporarily stationed in Hollywood, Florida, while waiting for orders to his first duty squadron. He met a local girl named Kay Ann Nixon, and they quickly fell in love. Although not formally engaged, the young couple discussed marriage when Kuhlman returned from his first overseas tour. Soon thereafter he received orders to head out to the Pacific Theater. He continued to correspond with Kay Ann after joining VP-101, and he wrote her a letter the morning of the October 1 mission.

Jake Nilva was involved with Jean Percy, a girl he had met in Perth. After the squadron shipped out to the war zone, Jake and Jean wrote to each other regularly. He even gave her his home address in St. Paul and suggested that she write to his family and introduce herself. Henry Zollinger corresponded regularly with a girl at home in Kentucky.

Of the eleven men aboard Jack Schenck's PBY on its night mission to Kendari, Harvey Harbecke was the champion in winning the young ladies. While in Australia he bought a Harley-Davidson motorcycle and used it to help attract the local girls. Like Bill Goodwin and Fred Warbois, Harbecke probably "liberated" a few gallons of aviation gas from the PBYs to run his vehicle. He had at least four girlfriends writing to his mother in America, with each of them telling her how wonderful her son "Duke" was. He must have left a long string of broken hearts behind him in Australia.

Chapter 3

Final Flights

Jack Schenck and his PBY crew moved out to the war zone in mid-1944 and began flying increasingly difficult missions. Executive Officer Lt. Joseph Gardner of squadron VP-101 called Schenck and his men well trained and one of his better crews. Schenck had more than fifteen hundred hours of Navy flying time under his belt by the end of September. Bill Goodwin had almost eleven hundred hours, and Art Kuhlman had about five hundred. Except for initial flight training, all these hours were in the PBY Catalina.

The men of the crew ranged in age from nineteen for Ray Cart and Paul Schilling to thirty-one for the old man of the group, Jake Nilva. Nilva looked even older, with prematurely white hair and the beginnings of baldness. The other crewmen were in their early- to mid-twenties.

This young, tight-knit crew was stationed on the Green and Admiralty Islands, both near the northeastern part of New Guinea. From late June until mid-September the crew flew rescue and antisubmarine patrols in the seas around Rabaul, the Japanese stronghold on the island of New Britain. When Allied air forces attacked the base, PBY Catalinas would circle nearby and await a radio call about any downed Allied planes. Schenck and his men rescued a New Zealand pilot a few miles off New Britain on

June 23, making a good open-sea landing and pulling the pilot safely aboard the PBY.

These lifesaving flights were called Dumbo missions because the PBY, with its big wings, reminded downed pilots of the Walt Disney cartoon character Dumbo, the flying elephant. The rescues could be difficult. As long as the seas were not too rough, the landings were usually successful. But if the Catalina landed too hard or hit a wave the wrong way, the impact could pop rivets from the hull or rip open the bottom. Many PBY crews who tried to land in heavy seas to rescue a downed airman ended up needing rescue themselves.

For pilot Bill Goodwin, a big break from the job of flying PBY missions came on August 20 when he took a leave to marry his Australian girlfriend. He had borrowed about $350 from ten of his fellow pilots in the squadron, and with this money in his pocket, he hopped a PBY flight to Brisbane, on Australia's eastern coast.

Valerie Storey obtained a special travel pass from the military and rode the train across the Australian continent to meet her boyfriend. On August 22, 1944, they were married in Brisbane's St. Stephen's Church. After a few days of honeymooning in Brisbane, Bill Goodwin went back to war. His eighteen-year-old bride, now pregnant, stood on a pier in Brisbane harbor and watched his PBY take off and head toward the war zone.

Goodwin rejoined Schenck's crew on September 2 and quickly repaid the money he had borrowed for his wedding. He kept a list of his creditors and the amounts due in a small notebook. As he paid his debts, he crossed out each of the names and the associated amounts.

On September 20 the squadron was ordered to Morotai. General MacArthur's forces had invaded the island five days earlier, and they were still fighting when four tenders anchored off shore in support of three American Black Cat squadrons—VP-11, VP-33, and VP-101—and elements of some Australian Black Cat squadrons. Schenck and his crew first bunked aboard the USS *San Carlos*. A few days later they moved to another tender, the USS

Tangier. From this point on, the main role changed for the crew and the rest of squadron VP-101. They stopped performing Dumbo rescues and began flying Black Cat night-attack missions.

From their new floating bases at Morotai, the Black Cats swept out to attack the Japanese in a wide arc from the Philippines in the north to Borneo in the west and down to the Celebes Islands in the southwest. VP-101 began sending out two or three Black Cats every night to find and attack Japanese shipping. Flights were timed so the black-painted PBYs arrived in enemy territory after dark and left before the sun rose.

Targets were plentiful. The PBYs found Japanese barges, luggers, and small freighters almost every night, and occasionally they located a destroyer or cruiser also. The Black Cats attacked the ships with everything they could carry: 500-pound and 100-pound bombs were dropped from under the wings, 23-pound parafrag bombs were dropped out the rear tunnel hatch by hand, .50 caliber machine guns fired from the two blister mounts on the sides of the plane, and .30 caliber machine guns fired from the nose and out the tunnel hatch.

On September 24, Schenck and his crew flew their first armed Black Cat night mission. They left Morotai around 7:00 P.M. and headed north. After entering enemy waters off the southern coast of the Philippine island of Mindanao, they patrolled for Japanese shipping using their radar and the sharp eyes of the lookouts. Later that night they spotted a group of Japanese barges and landing craft slowly moving across the sea. Schenck quickly attacked.

These vessels were too small to waste bombs on, so Schenck attacked with his plane's .30 and .50 caliber machine guns. An hour or so later they located another group of small craft and made six or seven strafing runs. Although their targets returned small-arms fire, no hits were made on the PBY that night. Later during their patrol they spotted a large, 8,000-ton freighter hiding in a river just above the coast. Before the PBY could attack, a rain squall hid the ship from view. The coming dawn and their decreasing fuel supply soon forced them to return to the base.

At 7:00 A.M. on September 25 they landed back at Morotai,

moored their PBY near the *Tangier*, and climbed aboard the tender for a debriefing, some food, and finally sleep. They were back home after spending twelve straight hours in the air and firing more than two thousand rounds of machine-gun ammunition at Japanese shipping. Of the two planes the squadron had sent out that night, the PBY manned by Schenck and his crew dealt the most damage to the enemy.

This operation was significant for all three pilots on Schenck's plane. Schenck had seen combat earlier in the New Guinea area during the squadron's second battle tour, when he had flown as the third pilot and later the second pilot in a PBY. But this combat mission was his first action against the enemy as a patrol plane commander. For Bill Goodwin and Art Kuhlman, it was the first taste of combat. Although Goodwin was a experienced pilot and had been in the Pacific Theater for more than a year, he had never really faced the enemy before. Kuhlman was new and relatively inexperienced, so this was a major milestone for him as well.

Goodwin thought his first combat significant enough to write a short narrative in the back of his logbook. He was so excited that he stayed up to describe it despite his exhaustion.

> This night I went on my first 'Black Cat' night operation against the enemy. We took off at Morotai 7:00 P.M. and went straight to Mindanao where we commenced searching for enemy ships and barges. We came upon one bunch of barges and landing boats which were moored and strafed them. We left to continue our search with two barges burning and one probably sinking. We continued on to Davao and found another concentration of small craft which we made six or seven strafing runs. A searchlight was turned on us here but turned right off. We sighted a 8000 ton ship in the river but before we could turn to make a bombing run a squall had covered it. Continuing the search we were shot at by shore battery but they did not hit us. The rest of the night was uneventful. We landed at our base at 0700 A.M. the 25th.

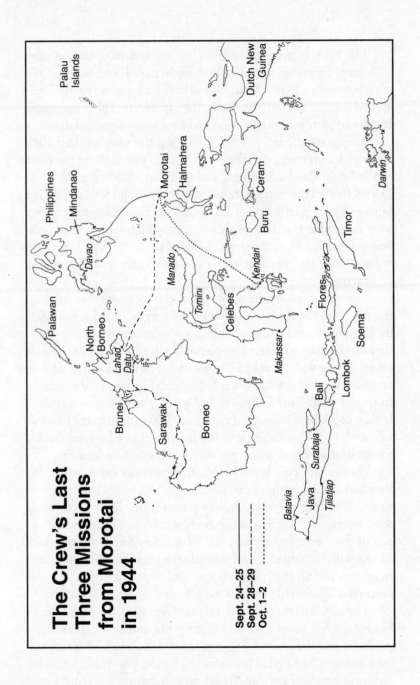

The Crew's Last
Three Missions
from Morotai
in 1944

Sept. 24–25 ————
Sept. 28–29 – – – –
Oct. 1–2 ·········

Palau
Islands

Dutch New
Guinea

Morotai
Halmahera
Ceram
Buru

Darwin

Philippines
Mindanao
Davao

Manado
Tomini
Celebes
Kendari

Timor

Palawan
North
Borneo
Lahad
Datu

Flores
Soema

Brunei
Sarawak
Borneo

Makassar

Bali
Lombok

Batavia
Java
Surabaja
Tjilatjap

The PBY crews needed time for rest and recuperation after each long, fatiguing, nerve-racking night patrol, and so it was not until September 28 that Schenck and his men went out again. Their second night mission would be the squadron's most successful Black Cat patrol during its third and final tour of combat duty.

They took off at 7:00 P.M., pointing the nose of their PBY westward. After nightfall they started their patrol along the coast of the huge island of Borneo, and at about 11:00 they flew into Darvel Bay on the northeastern coast of the island to check on the Japanese-held port town of Lahad Datu. Four enemy freighters were moored at the dock, which was piled high with war matériel being unloaded from the ships. Moored close by was a large concentration of barges. Schenck's decision to attack started a long and eventful battle.

The men opened the assault with a strafing attack that inflamed the stores on the dock and a few of the barges. Quickly they flew back out to sea and circled around for a second pass, during which they hit the dock with one 500-pound bomb and scored a near-miss on a freighter with another 500-pounder. The stores on the dock—ammunition and gasoline—exploded, causing fire and destruction to spread to all four freighters and a big warehouse nearby. Not letting up, Schenck dropped two more 500-pound bombs and all four of his 100-pounders into the inferno. Then he came back a fourth time and sank six barges with heavy machine-gun fire.

During the two-hour attack, the Japanese fired everything they had at the lone intruder. Enemy fire hit the PBY at least fifty times, knocking out the auxiliary power unit, slightly damaging one engine, and cutting some control cables. Miraculously, not one of the crewmembers was hit. When they finally headed back to sea with all ordnance expended, they left the four Japanese freighters and all the barges useless and the dock and warehouse destroyed. They could still see the fire seventy-five miles away.

The mission was so successful that Gen. Douglas MacArthur's headquarters released the story to the press, and newspapers across Australia and the United States printed it. Schenck later received the Distinguished Flying Cross for the attack. Everyone else on the crew was awarded the Air Medal, with Schilling receiving a gold star to add to an Air Medal he had won for a previous action with another crew.

In his logbook Schenck noted the damage to his plane: "50 holes in plane, 3 in fuel tanks, two in starboard engine, elevator controls severed." He logged the night's mission as taking 14.8 hours. The entry in the back of Jake Nilva's logbook best summed up the night's mission: "Our plane got holes in hull, engine, putt-putt, wing and elevator cable was shot away. NO ONE WAS HURT, THANK GOD!"

This daring attack revealed something about Jack Schenck: For a man who was fairly new at commanding a Black Cat night-attack mission, he seemed overconfident. The more experienced Black Cat pilots would sneak in on a target quickly and quietly, drop the bombs, and get out. Spending two hours over a target full of angry Japanese was asking for trouble.

"Bud" Smith, a radioman with one of the squadron's other plane crews, watched Schenck's PBY being hauled aboard the tender for repairs the next morning. After examining the fifty-some shell holes in the plane, he just walked away shaking his head in wonder. Word started to get around the squadron that Schenck was "gung ho," a wartime phrase that described men who were eager to charge into battle and be in on all the action. Jack Schenck was soon to get more than his share.

Schenck and his crew were scheduled to fly their third Black Cat night mission on Sunday, October 1. On the same day, their squadron's designation was changed from Patrol Squadron 101 (VP-101) to Patrol Bombing Squadron 29 (VPB-29). The crew also had a different plane, since the PBY they had used three days earlier was still being repaired. They climbed aboard PBY No. 08233 at about 5:00 P.M.

Their target area was the Japanese-held town of Kendari on the southeast coast of the Celebes. This remote, formerly peaceful little community was becoming a hot spot of war activity. In the half-month before Schenck's raid, four other PBYs had flown night missions to the Kendari area, looking for targets of opportunity. They found many.

Pilot Jim Merritt from squadron VP-33 had the most exciting

time. On the night of September 16, Lieutenant Merritt and his crew spotted a Japanese freighter in Kendari Harbor. He attacked low and released his bombs, hitting the ship but not sinking it. On his second pass he and his crew felt a sharp, heavy jolt throughout the PBY. After landing back at the tender the next morning, they found a piece of the mast tip from their target ship embedded in the wing's leading edge. They had come in so low that their wing had clipped the top off the ship's masthead.

On September 21, Lt. Comdr. Steve Johnson, commanding officer of VP-101, dropped several bombs at a Japanese destroyer escort near Kendari but missed his target. He nevertheless woke the Japanese defenders, who opened up with heavy, accurate anti-aircraft fire. Johnson quickly withdrew.

Four days later in Kendari Harbor Lt. Joe Gardner, VP-101's executive officer, attacked a small ship with a couple of 100-pound bombs and one thousand rounds of machine-gun fire. And on September 30, just one day before Schenck's mission, Lt. Gardner Burt of the same squadron strafed some barges in the harbor. All these PBYs reported heavy, accurate antiaircraft fire from the mouth of Kendari Harbor.

Perhaps the eleven men of PBY No. 08233 thought of their comrades' recent missions as they flew to Kendari. Arriving off the coast near the town, they started the search for enemy shipping, and around 1:00 A.M., they found a likely target in the harbor. The plane's radio operator contacted the squadron base and gave their location in code. He then began transmitting the letter "A" in Morse code continuously (dit-dah, dit-dah, dit-dah . . .). Standard procedure was to transmit the letter "A" throughout an attack, then send an "OK" when the attack was over.

Schenck flew in for the attack. Back at the base, an operator heard the Morse code "A's" transmitting steadily from the plane. Then they stopped, without the customary "OK" message. After a long pause, the base received a message: "One man wounded, control cable shot. Am returning to base from Kendari." That was it. No more messages were received.

Chapter 4

Bushido

The airmen who flew against the Japanese feared capture more than being killed outright in combat. During the fighting in Europe, the Axis forces took more than 95,000 Americans as prisoners and about 1 percent of them died in captivity. Of the 34,600 Americans known to have been taken prisoner in the Pacific, over 37 percent died while in the hands of the Japanese. In other words, if a U.S. soldier were captured by the Japanese, his chances of not coming home were about one in three. The actual numbers of prisoners and those who died are probably higher than listed because many Americans were captured and killed without being reported as prisoners.

The Japanese particularly disliked Allied airmen, who seemed to suffer more than other prisoners. The poor treatment of captured airmen began in April 1942, when the United States struck against the home islands of Japan. Army Air Corps Col. James Doolittle led sixteen B-25 Army bombers off a Navy carrier and bombed Tokyo, Osaka, and Nagoya. None of the planes were shot down, but all were lost when they ran out of gas while trying to reach friendly forces in China. Eight of the B-25 airmen were captured by the Japanese Army in China.

The Japanese were so upset by the bombing of their homeland

that they devised the Enemy Airmen's Law, which went into effect August 13, 1942, giving them a pretext for punishing any Allied airmen they captured. The law simply stated that anyone who bombed or strafed nonmilitary targets was guilty of war crimes and would be punished accordingly. In practice, it did not seem to matter what the target actually was; the Japanese would simply declare it nonmilitary and retaliate against captured airmen. The Japanese had no qualms of their own about bombing nonmilitary targets; they had been doing so since invading China in the 1930s.

The eight prisoners from the Doolittle raid were tried in a kangaroo court under the new law, despite the fact it was put into effect four months after their bombing mission. Although they had bombed only legitimate military targets, three of the prisoners were sentenced to death and executed. The remaining five were sentenced to life in prison, but were released at the war's end.

This vengeful attitude set the precedent for treatment of captured Allied airmen for the rest of the war. Of the thousands of Allied airmen seized by the Japanese, only a handful survived to tell their tales. All Allied air crews were briefed on what to expect if shot down and taken alive. They all understood that if captured, they would probably be on the receiving end of a bullet, bayonet or, more than likely, the Japanese samurai sword.

During the war, Naval Intelligence circulated among some PBY squadrons captured Japanese photographs showing Allied airmen about to be beheaded in hopes of identifying the victims. A Black Cat PBY from VP-33 with a crew of nine commanded by Lt. (jg) Russ Childs had been shot down off Hollandia (now Djajapura) on the northern coast of Dutch New Guinea on March 12, 1944. No trace was ever found of the crew, but it was rumored they were captured and quickly beheaded. The execution pictures being circulated were thought to be of members of Childs's crew, but they were too blurry for positive identification.

Most airmen carried a sidearm on missions over enemy territory, and many said they would use the pistol on themselves rather than be captured by the Japanese. Suicide would be better than being shown "the way of Bushido" by their Japanese captors.

Bushido, the code of the samurai warrior, was an ancient Japanese system of conduct and behavior. As a religion and philosophy, Bushido dictated the life of the ruling class for centuries. The samurai, who held themselves above the daily work of the common people, split their time between the arts of war and the cultured arts, such as calligraphy, poetry, writing, and painting.

One of the philosophies of Bushido was the concept of compassion in battle and compassion for the enemy—a type of compassion that is almost incomprehensible to the Western mind. When a samurai warrior was seriously wounded in battle, one of his fellow soldiers would show compassion by cutting off the warrior's head and hiding it so that it would not fall into the hands of the enemy. When a samurai warrior shamed himself or failed in a task, he could redeem himself by committing *seppuku*, or *hara-kiri* (belly splitting). When the dying man had cut open his belly enough to satisfy honor and tradition, his assistant would show compassion by cutting off the head of the dying man so that he would not suffer too long. It was considered a great honor to die by having your head removed with a samurai sword.

One Japanese soldier, who had just witnessed the beheading of an Allied airman in the South Pacific, noted in his diary his feelings about the beheading.

> All is over. The head is dead white like a doll's. The savageness which I felt only a little while ago is gone, and now I feel nothing but the true compassion of Japanese Bushido.

The samurai lost their position of power in the eighteenth century as the country unified and moved into the modern world. Bushido almost died out. In the latter part of the nineteenth century, Japan's military rulers revived parts of the code to instill obedience, discipline, and fighting spirit in their subjects. By the 1930s the entire nation accepted the revised code.

To Japan's military, Bushido was almost a religion. It developed in close association with Shinto and Buddhism, the main religions of the Japanese. Modern Bushido stressed obedience to the emperor above all else. A military order from a superior was the same as an order from the emperor himself—it was to be obeyed without question.

Always adhering strictly to the code of Bushido, the Japanese soldier or sailor refused to retreat from the enemy or to surrender. He was expected to die in battle or to kill himself if there was a chance that he would be taken prisoner. To become a prisoner of war was to disgrace oneself, one's family, the nation and, most importantly, the emperor.

Allied forces quickly learned that the Japanese fighting man would rather die than surrender. When Allied forces invaded a Japanese-held island, almost all the Japanese troops would die in the subsequent fighting. On the tiny island of Tarawa almost five thousand defending Japanese fought to the death and, in doing so, killed one thousand Americans and wounded two thousand more.

Because of their military code, the Japanese had nothing but contempt for the Allied prisoners they captured during the Pacific war. They could not comprehend the Western practice of surrendering to the enemy when the battle was lost, which may be why the Japanese treated POWs so terribly.

Allied prisoners were often forced to march in a humiliating parade before local populations throughout Asia. The Japanese thought it important to show the inferiority of Western civilization to people of their new "Greater East Asia Co-Prosperity Sphere." They thought this so important to their propaganda efforts that they even moved Allied captives into occupied areas that had no prisoners of war, such as Korea.

War crimes investigations held in China after the war revealed the hideous torture that Allied prisoners received. Lt. Toru Miki was one of the Japanese Army officers running a prison camp in Manchuria. An American sailor, William B. Jones, was held in the camp, and in November 1943, he invoked the wrath of Miki. The war crimes report stated that Jones

. . . was working in the local factory and machine shop, and had secured some cigarettes from a Chinese workman. He was searched at the gate, taken to the superintendent's office and beaten by the accused [Miki] with a wooden club. Jones' face was a mass of bruises and cuts, badly swollen and discolored. He was bleeding from the nose, mouth and from several cuts. Jones who was a big and husky man was then thrown into the "brig," and later transferred to the hospital where he died of "pneumonia" on 20 November 1943. The accused nearly always carried this club with him and seemed to delight in hitting someone with it.

An extreme example of Japan's barbaric treatment of prisoners is the story of Maj. Sueo Matoba of the Japanese Imperial Army. Matoba controlled Allied prisoners on the small, little-known Pacific island of Chichi-shima. A number of American airmen fell into his hands, but none survived for long. He used POWs for the live bayonet practice of his troops or simply beheaded them. Further, Matoba butchered their bodies and cooked the pieces; then he fed the human flesh to his unwitting subordinates as a big joke. After the war Matoba was tried for these hideous crimes and found guilty. He was hanged in 1947.

The execution of prisoners by the Japanese commonly occurred across the Pacific, and there are documented cases of as many as 120 newly captured prisoners being put to death at the same time. Sometimes entire units that surrendered in good faith were massacred soon after laying down their arms.

Mass murder was not limited to military prisoners. Hospital patients were killed along with complete staffs, from the head of the hospital down to the lowest orderly. Early in the Pacific war, the Japanese Navy issued a standing order that the crews of merchant ships sunk by Japanese submarines were to be prevented from returning to service. To Japanese sailors, this meant killing the ships' crews, and they soon extended this policy to include civilian

passengers, both men and women, as well. After a Japanese sub-
marine sank a merchant ship, it would surface and machine-gun the
survivors. On occasion they would interrogate a few survivors, then
kill them one by one and throw their bodies overboard. The sub
crews used swords, guns, sledgehammers, wrenches, and anything
else at hand to murder their helpless victims. They even seemed to
take delight in their gruesome task. Somehow a few victims survived this senseless murder, were rescued by passing ships, and
were able to tell their horrible story.

From the earliest days of the war to its end, the Allies protested
the cruel treatment of prisoners, channeling their objections through
neutral countries. The Japanese usually ignored the protests or dis-
missed them as being exaggerated.

The brutal treatment of prisoners, although nearly universal
throughout the Japanese military during the war, was not the official stated policy of the Japanese government. From the beginning,
the government of Japan promised to treat prisoners of war decently.
A few days after Japan's attack on Pearl Harbor, the United States
secretary of state, Cordell Hull, sent the following message to the
Japanese through neutral Switzerland:

> It is the intention of the Government of the United
> States as a party to the Geneva Prisoner of War Con-
> vention and the Geneva Red Cross Convention, both of
> July 27, 1929, to apply the provisions of those Conven-
> tions. It is, furthermore, the intention of the Government
> of the United States to apply the provisions of the Geneva
> Prisoner of War Convention to any civilian enemy aliens
> that may be interned, in so far as the provisions of that
> convention may be adaptable thereto. Although the
> Japanese Government is a signatory of the above con-
> ventions, it is understood not to have ratified the Geneva
> Prisoner of War Convention. The Government of the
> United States nevertheless hopes that the Japanese
> Government will apply the provisions of both conven-
> tions reciprocally in the above sense. The Government

of the United States would appreciate receiving an expression of the intentions of the Japanese Government in the respect.

The Japanese, also through the Swiss, officially replied a few weeks later with a brief note:

Japan is strictly observing Geneva Red Cross Convention as a signatory state. Although not bound by the (Geneva Prisoner of War) Convention relative treatment prisoners of war Japan will apply mutatis mutandis provisions of that Convention to American Prisoners of War in its power.

Mutatis mutandis means reciprocal treatment between countries; if America treated its prisoners according to the provisions of both conventions, Japan would do the same. The only problem was that this response was crafted by diplomats, not the military leaders who held the real power and who controlled the prisoners of war.

The Japanese military had a set of written rules that was designed to govern the treatment of war captives. Rikutatsu (Regulation) No. 22, dated February 14, 1904, along with its revisions and additions, was the Japanese military's official policy on handling prisoners of war. But very few military personnel in the field knew anything about Rikutatsu No. 22. History would prove that the Japanese hardly ever followed their own regulations regarding prisoners of war, let alone international rules and laws.

Chapter 5

Captured!

During the early morning hours of October 2, 1944, squadron VPB-29's radio operators tried repeatedly to reestablish communications with Jack Schenck's plane, without success. When the PBY did not return at first light as scheduled, it was listed as missing. Army and Navy search planes explored Schenck's patrol area but found no trace of the missing PBY. Navy officials soon called off the search and officially declared the men of PBY No. 08233 missing in action.

Their squadron mates assumed they were dead. With no further radio messages from the crew and no sight of them from the air, the men of VPB-29 believed that the plane went down at sea with the loss of all hands. The family of each missing man soon received the dreaded telegram from the Navy Department. The one sent to William and Catherine Goodwin was typical:

> The Navy Department deeply regrets to inform you that your son Lieutenant (Junior Grade) William Francis Goodwin Junior USNR is missing in action 1 October 1944 while in the service of his country. The Department appreciates your great anxiety but details not now available and delay in receipt thereof must necessarily

be expected. To prevent possible aid to our enemies
please do not divulge the name of his ship or station.

Vice Admiral Randall Jacobs
The Chief of Naval Personnel

Nevertheless, nine of the eleven men on Schenck's PBY did
not die on October 2. The plane did not crash far out at sea; it
crash-landed within sight of a tiny island called Umbele, in the
Salabangka Islands just off the coast of the main island of the
Celebes, and about fifty miles north of Kendari. When the badly
damaged plane finally came to rest on the water, Jack Schenck and
Art Kuhlman were dead, either as a result of enemy fire or, more
likely, from the crash landing.

Lt. Bill Goodwin suddenly found himself in command of the
eight remaining crewmen. Under his direction the survivors
grabbed what they could from the plane and abandoned it. A PBY,
being little more than a boat hull with wings, can stay afloat in-
definitely if it has no holes below the waterline. Their PBY floated
long enough for the survivors to throw their life raft out of one of
the open blisters, pack it with emergency gear, pull their two dead
companions out of the plane and into the raft, and paddle away.
The plane then sank, either from enemy shell holes or from care-
fully placed gunshots fired by crew members as they abandoned it.
Crew members had been trained to scuttle a PBY if they were
forced to land in enemy territory.

Umbele was not much more than a large, barren rock—not a
good place for the crew to bury their dead, and a worse place to
hide from the Japanese. The men quickly decided to head toward a
bigger island not far away. They pushed away from the sinking
plane, paddled to the tree-covered island of Bungkinkela, and
landed in a small cove called Tanjung Lepe. They hid in the jungle
some distance from the little village of Paku. They did not know it
then, but they had been spotted by some of the natives who lived
in Paku.

The men quickly took stock of their situation. They had some food and water from the raft's survival kit, an emergency radio, a first aid kit, a few pistols and carbines, charts of the area, and the clothes they were wearing. Jake Nilva had suffered a bad gash across his nose from one of the antiaircraft hits that damaged the PBY. Except for minor cuts and scratches, the other eight were in good shape.

The stranded airmen buried Schenck and Kuhlman and tried to contact friendly forces with their emergency radio. Every PBY carried an emergency radio, which was affectionately called a "Gibson girl" by some because of its hourglass shape. Others referred to it as "the coffee grinder" because a user had to crank a handle on top, just like an old-fashioned coffee mill, to generate electrical power.

The small yellowish-orange radio could transmit but not receive. A downed airman clamped it tightly between his knees at the narrow part of its hourglass shape and held it firmly in place with a large strap around his thighs. He would then crank furiously to transmit a signal. The Gibson girl continually transmitted a preset SOS message on 500 kilocycles and 8,364 kilocycles, the international emergency frequencies. The radio could also be switched to manual so that any message could be tapped out in Morse code at those same frequencies.

Since the men had the radio transmitter and three experienced radio operators in Sommer, McMaster, and Zollinger, they must have tried very hard to get a message out but apparently were unsuccessful. About 600 miles from the closest friendly base, their Gibson girl was transmitting at its stated maximum range, and the radio signals could have traveled that far or farther under the right atmospheric conditions. But conditions could have been bad, limiting the effective range of the signals. It is also possible that their Gibson girl was not working.

A chance to make contact with friendly forces came two nights after the crew was shot down. Lt. John Zubler flew into the Kendari area on a Black Cat night mission. He knew a PBY had gone down in the area, and he and his crew looked for their comrades, actually coming within a few miles of the stranded men.

Zubler might have picked up emergency signals as he flew near Kendari had not one of his radiomen been killed, two other crewmen wounded, and his plane shot up. As hard as Goodwin and his men must have tried to reach someone on their emergency radio, no friendly forces ever heard their distress calls.

Although the American airmen stranded on the island of Bungkinkela were deep in enemy territory, they had actually landed in what should have been a relatively safe location. No Japanese forces were stationed on any of the Salabangka Islands or on the adjacent Celebes mainland.

Two or three days after coming ashore, the Americans made contact with Pai, a local fisherman. They spotted him fishing in the waters near their hiding place and tried to get him to come closer. After much coaxing Pai finally came ashore. They communicated with broken English and hand gestures until Pai understood that they wanted him to take them to his village. They wanted to see the local officials but not the Japanese.

The Americans had no way of knowing whether they could trust the natives. If they had been shot down in New Guinea, the Solomon Islands, or the Philippines, they could have looked to the native population for help. The local population in areas occupied by the Japanese had aided hundreds of Allied soldiers, sailors, and airmen. The airmen hoped for the same type of helpful treatment in the Celebes.

Unknown to them, their sudden appearance set frenzied activities in motion on the nearby island of Salabangka. Shortly after the Americans had pulled their life boat ashore, the villagers of Paku sent a messenger over to Salabangka. The messenger, a local man named Abdul Rijai, reported the landing of the Americans to the native headman, H. Komendangi. Komendangi was a well-educated district attorney under Dutch rule. He had been elevated to district head by the Japanese, who considered him dependable and sympathetic to their cause. It was in his best interests to do anything he could to keep himself in good standing with the Japanese.

Komendangi immediately set out to capture the Americans and turn them over to the Japanese. He disguised a small group of trusted men as fishermen and set off for Paku in fishing boats. On Bungkinkela he teamed up with the Paku village chief, M. Rivai.

The two Indonesians contacted the Americans, making a show of friendship and somehow convincing the airmen that they were on their side. Komendangi and Rivai lured the nine men to Paku with the promise of food, shelter, and help. They made them feel at home in Paku, allowing them to stay in the local communal hut.

The Americans were still armed with several pistols and carbines, so Komendangi and Rivai left them alone for a few days. The Americans soon let their guard down. One night as the airmen slept, Komendangi and his men jumped them and took their guns. The surprised Americans fought back fiercely with fists, elbows, knees, feet, and teeth. Though much bigger than the slightly built Indonesian attackers, the white men were far outnumbered. They were soon overwhelmed and tied up. Their freedom in enemy territory had lasted only five or six days.

Komendangi loaded the captives in his fishing boats the next day and took them to Salabangka. Komendangi would later receive a medal from the Japanese, which prompted him to stage a big celebration to show off the medal and expound on his great adventure.

When Komendangi and Rivai set out to capture the fliers, they sent a report to the Japanese naval base at Kendari on the PBY's crash landing and its survivors. The base commander, Capt. Gosuke Taniguchi, quickly dispatched a motorboat with about ten men, led by Ensign Sazae Chiuma, to capture the airmen and bring them to Kendari.

Taniguchi also radioed the information to his superior, Vice Adm. Morikazu Ohsugi, in the city of Makassar, about 250 miles west of Kendari on the other side of the southwest finger of the Celebes. Admiral Ohsugi sent a small floatplane to help in the search. The floatplane stopped briefly in Kendari for orders and then flew on to the Salabangka area to meet up with Chiuma.

While all this activity was taking place, another Japanese officer from the Kendari naval base, Ensign Seijiro Dan, happened to be farther up the coast from the Salabangka Islands. Dan was at Dungpu, looking for a good location to place a new radar installation. While heading back to Kendari in his motorboat *Daikeku Maru,* Dan passed between the Salabangka Islands and the mainland. Komendangi spotted Dan's boat, and he quickly loaded his American prisoners into a fishing boat and took them out to Dan. To his great surprise, Dan received nine captured American Navy airmen from Komendangi. Dan immediately took the prisoners into custody, loaded them onto the *Daikeku Maru,* and headed for Kendari.

Meanwhile, Ensign Chiuma and his men were searching the Salabangka Islands for the Americans. The floatplane found Chiuma's boat and landed nearby. Chiuma climbed aboard the floatplane and flew around the area, looking unsuccessfully for any sign of the airmen or their crashed plane. After landing back at Salabangka, he learned from Komendangi that Ensign Dan already had the Americans in custody and was on his way to Kendari. Chiuma ordered his men back to Kendari in the motorboat while he flew to Kendari in the floatplane.

Chiuma immediately reported to Captain Taniguchi at Kendari. Taniguchi sent a written message back to Makassar with the returning floatplane, requesting that an English-speaking interpreter be sent to help interrogate the Americans who would soon arrive. He followed up the written message with a radio request for an interpreter.

Ensign Dan's boat carrying the captured Americans reached Kendari and tied up to the dock about 4:00 P.M. on October 8, 1944. It was almost a week since Jack Schenck and Art Kuhlman had died in the crash of PBY No. 08233 and the nine survivors had paddled ashore. They were now prisoners of the Japanese.

Chapter 6

Kendari

The mistreatment and killing of Allied prisoners of war at Kendari started the day the town was invaded by the Empire of Japan. The invaders needed only a few hours on January 24, 1942, to secure the town and the area around it. During this short fight, Johan Tomasawa and eleven other Dutch-trained Indonesian soldiers were captured. Later that day, the Japanese brought in thirty-six U.S. Navy prisoners picked up from a warship they had sunk.

The Americans and Indonesians were put in the Dutch Guard House that would soon become the prison compound. They were taken out a few at a time for questioning by the highest-ranking Japanese present, Teitje Nakamura. After all had been interrogated, they were lined up on the parade ground of the newly captured Dutch Army camp. Nakamura called the names of seventeen Americans, who stepped forward one by one. The Japanese tied the men's hands behind their backs and loaded them into trucks. Johan Tomasawa and his eleven fellow Indonesian prisoners went in another truck, and Nakamura and his staff rode in a car. The little convoy traveled a few miles to the village of Amoito.

At Amoito the twelve Indonesian prisoners were ordered to dig three large holes. At each hole Nakamura stationed a Japanese officer with a drawn sword. At the orders of Nakamura, the Americans were blindfolded, brought forward, and forced to kneel. They were then beheaded, and their bodies were thrown into the graves. The Indonesians were ordered to fill in the graves. The remaining American prisoners in Kendari were held for about two weeks and then shipped off to work as laborers in nickel mines on the island.

The next recorded killings at Kendari took place during the first week of June 1942. A couple of weeks earlier, the Japanese Navy sank a British merchant ship off Tjilatjap, Java. The seventeen survivors included ten white men, four Malays, and three Chinese, who were pulled from the sea by the Japanese and brought to the Kendari prison compound, run by the Japanese Navy agency Tokkei Tai. The Tokkei Tai, the equivalent of the Japanese Army's infamous Kempi Tai, performed the combined functions of a military police force and a secret police. Their presence led to the prison's being referred to by their name.

History repeated itself as their captors loaded these seventeen men into trucks and drove them to Amoito. Two new graves were dug about ten feet from those of the seventeen Americans killed in January. As before, Japanese soldiers tied and blindfolded their victims, led them to the side of the graves, and beheaded them. With the war in the Pacific only six months old, the Japanese in the quiet little town of Kendari had already taken at least thirty-four innocent lives.

Evidence developed after the war shows that other victims of the Japanese in Kendari were not as lucky as those beheaded. Some were tortured to death within the Tokkei Tai. A report on suspected war crimes in Kendari written a few months after the war describes how some prisoners held in the Tokkei Tai prison were killed:

> Three Allied spies, two natives and an Arab, were caught sending radio messages to Allies. They were tortured to death. First burned by fire on the buttocks, then rolled over glowing embers and finally rolled over barbed wire. We were told about a method of torture practiced by the Japs, and inspected the place where this took place. Victims were strapped on to a bamboo bed, and a fire lighted underneath. The bed was there

at the date of writing with a hole in the centre, two feet
long by a foot wide (approx) and charred and blackened
by fire, and beneath on the cement floor was a blackened
patch where the fire had obviously been placed.

After the war, Allied investigators found bloody fingerprints
and smears of blood on the walls of some of the Tokkei Tai cells.
When investigators asked about this blood, the Japanese replied
that "the men's faces were bleeding from mosquito bites and they
wiped their faces with their hands, and then wiped their hands on
the walls." The investigators reported that they did not believe the
Japanese explanation.

This report also cited a number of Allied airmen who were
probably killed after being captured. Investigators could not find
names or dates, but they heard about four Allied airmen brought
from Boetong Island to Kendari for execution. It was rumored
that the Japanese captured an Allied captain at Pomala sometime
in 1943 and executed him at Kendari. In yet another instance, an
American P-38 pilot was said to have crashed at Komda. He was
captured and killed five days later at the Kendari airfield.

Harry Mesman, a local Indonesian working as a driver and
mechanic for the Japanese at Kendari, told Allied investigators after
the war that two of the Japanese from the Tokkei Tai—named Abe
and Tooru Tanaka—had killed and buried thirty-three natives in
Kendari.

Except for the Japanese invasion and the Allied air raids near
the end of the conflict, little Kendari was pretty much bypassed
during the war. Yet a large number of Allied military personnel
and local civilians met their deaths in and around Kendari at the
hands of the Japanese invaders.

After the war, the Graves Registration team in Kendari found
several graves containing more than one hundred bodies. War
crimes investigators referred to the Kendari area as the "Japanese
execution grounds."

It was now October 1944, and the Japanese at Kendari held nine
new American prisoners. The Japanese involved with the nine

American airmen were, on the average, much older than their captives. With a few exceptions, these Japanese fell in two groups. The first were the older, high-ranking, well-educated, and experienced professional naval officers who had achieved senior positions after many years of active service. The others were the junior officers who had previously been noncommissioned officers and had been promoted to officer rank because of the heavy losses suffered by the Japanese Navy in the Pacific war.

These junior officers, like Sazae Chiuma and Tooru Tanaka, had started out as ordinary seamen and after years of hard, even brutal, service in the Imperial Navy had risen to the rank of senior noncommissioned officer or warrant officer. From there many were given commissions. Had it not been for the war, they would probably never have reached the lofty position of commissioned officer. Ensign Chiuma was thirty-three, while Lt. (jg) Bill Goodwin was one rank higher but only twenty-four years old at the time of his capture.

Vice Adm. Morikazu Ohsugi, a fifty-two-year-old career officer, started his naval career in 1910 after graduating from Eta Jima, Japan's Naval Academy. He took over command of the 23rd Special Naval Base Unit in Makassar, Celebes Islands, in January 1944. From there he commanded all of southwestern and southeastern Celebes, including the Kendari Naval Base, a subgroup of the 23rd Naval Base Unit. The only exception to this control was the Kendari Naval Air Base, which was commanded by Rear Adm. Tamotsu Furukawa.

Capt. Gosuke Taniguchi arrived in the Celebes in August 1944. In Kendari he commanded the transportation unit that shipped supplies to the Japanese 4th Southern Area Fleet headquartered on the island of Ambon, southeast of Kendari. Just before Jack Schenck and his crew attacked the Harbor, the captain took on the added responsibility of command of the Kendari Naval Base along with its Tokkei Tai agency and prison compound. Taniguchi was a fifty-one-year-old career naval officer with more than thirty years of service. He and his superior, Admiral Ohsugi, had known each other since their days together at the naval academy.

Another graduate of Eta Jima, Rear Adm. Tamotsu Furukawa was commissioned an ensign in the Japanese Navy in December 1915. The naval aviator took command of the 23rd Naval Air Flotilla near Kendari about the time Captain Taniguchi obtained full command of the Kendari garrison. The naval air base was officially designated a combat-ready air unit, but by the time the nine Americans were brought in, Furukawa had few combat planes left.

Admiral Furukawa's chief of staff at the air base, Capt. Takao Sonokawa, was a career naval officer. In the beginning of September 1944, at age forty-four, he was transferred from Tokyo to the Kendari Naval Air Base. Captain Sonokawa was to become deeply involved in the interrogation of the nine American airmen.

Another career naval officer, Capt. Yoshiotsu Moritama, was assigned to the Naval Air Base in July 1944. The fifty-year-old reported directly to Admiral Furukawa and commanded the *gohoku*, or maintenance unit, of the 23rd Naval Air Unit. Though responsible for maintaining the naval aircraft and associated equipment, Moritama and his fifteen hundred men had very little to maintain because of aircraft losses and bomb damage.

Ten years younger than Moritama, Lt. (jg) Keiichi Nozaka had joined the Japanese Navy in 1923 and worked his way up from enlisted man to officer because of the war. After his promotion to lieutenant (junior grade), he went to Kendari to command the 53rd Antiaircraft Unit stationed around the airfield. By war's end Nozaka had been promoted to full lieutenant.

At twenty-five, Lt. (jg) Toshio Mitani was an exception to other junior officers since he was the appropriate age for his rank. He led a regular platoon in the Landing Patrol Section of the Kendari garrison. Although his immediate superior was Lt. Saburo Takita, commander of the Tokkei Tai, he had no actual connection with the Tokkei Tai.

The prison compound, which the Japanese referred to simply as the Tokkei Tai, was under the direct command of Lt. Saburo Takita but was actually run by a Chief Warrant Officer whose last name was Abe. Takita reported directly to Captain Taniguchi, the base commander, and he was also Taniguchi's executive officer.

Ensign Sazae Chiuma's position in the Tokkei Tai chain of command was between Takita and Abe.

Chiuma was thirty-three when he controlled the nine Americans in the Tokkei Tai. He commanded twelve warrant officers, six noncommissioned officers, and three civilian interpreters who spoke the local languages. Chiuma also led a heavy weapons platoon in the regular Kendari garrison. If Kendari ever was attacked by Allied forces, Chiuma would have abandoned his duties at the prison compound and fought as a foot soldier.

Even under the circumstances, at thirty-seven Ensign Seijiro Dan was old for an ensign. He had started his naval career as an enlisted seaman in 1927, and he worked up to the commissioned rank of ensign and became a skilled communications officer. Dan was assigned to the Kendari garrison on October 30, 1943, and stayed there until the war ended.

In contrast, Ensign Tokioka Maeda was a relatively young naval officer, having started his career in 1943 as a cadet. At twenty-three he was commissioned an ensign and stationed in the Kendari area with the 53rd Antiaircraft Unit, which protected the airfield. He spent his entire military career in Kendari.

Ensign Yoshitaka Ogawa, thirty-two, was a platoon leader of the motor section for the Kendari garrison. His section maintained all the vehicles and welded and repaired large equipment for the Kendari Naval Base. Ogawa had joined the Navy in 1929 as a regular seaman.

Another enlisted sailor who had received a commission, Ensign Isokichi Yamamoto, thirty-three, had been in the Navy since 1928. He was assigned as a platoon leader in the Kendari garrison.

In April 1942 Chief Petty Officer Tooru Tanaka, thirty-one, arrived at Kendari. He had been inducted into the Navy as a seaman recruit in October 1941 and quickly worked his way up in rank. He was initially assigned to Kendari's antiaircraft unit, but in July of the following year, he was assigned to the Tokkei Tai, where he remained until the war's end. By the time the Japanese surrendered, Tanaka had risen to the rank of ensign.

A thirty-year-old civilian police inspector had been assigned to work for the military police in Kendari. Torao Sato investigated civilian cases, performed counterintelligence, and occasionally worked on the cases of disobedient Japanese military personnel. He arrived in Kendari and reported for duty a few days before Schenck's PBY was shot down.

These were the men who captured and controlled the nine American fliers and who would determine their fate. Life as a prisoner of war under these soldiers would be hazardous if they were typical Japanese military men.

Chapter 7

Interrogation

When Ensign Dan's motorboat arrived at Kendari with his nine American prisoners, Captain Taniguchi ordered Ensign Chiuma to ensure that his men locked the captives in the small prison compound. The nine airmen were now among the approximately three thousand American, British, Dutch, and Australian prisoners being held in the Celebes Islands.

Most of the Allied prisoners were in a camp just outside the Celebes main city of Makassar (now called Ujung Pandang). The Japanese government never notified the Allies through the International Red Cross that these prisoners were being held, and their existence was not known until the war ended. All three thousand were listed as missing in action and thought to be dead.

At the dock Chiuma's men shoved the nine Americans into the back of an old truck and drove them to the Tokkei Tai compound, which had twelve cells. Abe took charge of the prisoners and locked each one in a separate cell.

Chiuma confiscated their few belongings, including a piece of electronic gear that he thought was an Identification Friend or Foe (IFF) set. But the IFF unit of the PBY was far too big to remove from the plane in an emergency—and in any case, it was something the Americans would have destroyed rather than let fall into enemy hands. The gear Chiuma took must have been their emergency transmitter, the Gibson girl radio. One of the first things Chiuma, Taniguchi, and an interpreter asked the Americans was about the "use and workings of the wireless equipment they had with them."

Chiuma also confiscated money, rings, watches, identification bracelets, notebooks, and photos of the men's girlfriends and families. He inventoried the items and turned them over to Taniguchi, who locked them in his safe and sent the list to his superior, Admiral Ohsugi, in Makassar.

Shortly after the Americans were locked in their cells, Warrant Officer Abe questioned each of them with the help of a local Indonesian, Yohn Tjio, who could speak English. After the war Tjio related his brief encounter with the Americans to Allied investigators.

> Q: *Did you see any American prisoners of war at or about this time?*
> A: Yes.
> Q: *Tell what you know concerning them.*
> A: In October 1944 I lived in the house of one Kannang, who was a teacher or gooru [guru]. On October 8th he told me that while I was out a Jap soldier from the Tokkei Tai was there looking for me—so I went to Tokkei Tai headquarters. There I was asked if I could speak English—I told the officer "a little." I was then told to wait, that some captured American PBY flyers who had been brought down near Salabangka were being brought by motor-boat to Kendari, and that I was to act as interpreter. . . . The boat arrived and the Americans were brought to Tokkei Tai Headquarters in a truck. Captain Taniguchi was standing outside the headquarters with other Japanese officers when the prisoners arrived.
> Q: *Did Taniguchi personally speak to any of the prisoners?*
> A: He did not.
> Q: *Did he direct you to ask any questions?*

A: He did not. Taniguchi never spoke to the Americans at all, and when they were brought inside for questioning he remained outside.

Q: *Can you describe these prisoners as best you can?*

A: I have written a description of them on a separate sheet which I would like to have attached to this statement.

Q: *What happened after the Americans were taken in the headquarters?*

A: Under the direction of Abe, I questioned each one of the Americans individually and separately—as to their name, age, rank, station from which they came, etc. The questioning lasted about one and a half hours. When the last man was questioned, Abe went out, and I followed shortly thereafter. I took notes during the questioning. . . . In the group of Americans, I think there was one officer—a Lieutenant Goodwin—fair eyes, dark straight hair, tall and thin. One was injured—he had a cut across the bridge of his nose—it had already been bandaged when I saw him. One of the men was John Sommer. One of the Americans told me that they were navy flyers, that they were in a PBY plane. That it had crashed in the sea about 1 A.M.—off the Island of Salabangka— that two of the eleven members of the crew had died in the crash.

The following is Tjio's written description—not totally accurate—of the prisoners as he saw them the day they arrived in Kendari:

> 1. Lft Goodwin—not very tall, a little bit thin, age 24, dark eyes, a brown service suit, without shoes, flat hair. [Bill Goodwin]
> 2. Yohn Summers—Tall & thin, age 21, hair color reddish (chestnut), blue navy suit, straight nose, no other marks. [Joe Sommer]

3. Short, a little fat, an injury on his nose, waving hair, blue suit and age 32. [Jake Nilva]

4. Tall, well built, brown waving hair, age 26, blue navy suit. [Harvey Harbecke]

5. Thin and tall, brown hair, blue navy suit and age 19. [Paul Schilling]

6. Short, fat, curly hair, fair eyes, blue navy suit and age 23. [Henry Zollinger]

7. Short, a little bit fat, dark curly hair, blue navy suit, age 21. [Raymond Cart]

8. Tall, thin, brown hair, blue navy suit, fair eyes, age 20. [Edwin McMaster]

9. Strong and tall man, black hair, blue navy suit, age 22. [Walter Price]

From Tjio's statement one cannot tell whether Abe used any force during this initial questioning. In all probability he did, since Abe was not known for kind treatment of prisoners.

The next day Captain Taniguchi arrived to interrogate the new prisoners himself. He could read, write, and speak English. Prison guards took the Americans out of their cells one at a time and brought them to the interrogation room at the front of the Tokkei Tai compound. Taniguchi asked each man his name, rank, and unit and where the PBY flew from on its last mission. They must have answered some of his questions, for he learned that they had come from the United States by way of Australia before moving out to the war zone and that they had flown from Morotai on their final mission.

After this round of interrogations, Taniguchi wrote a preliminary report and radioed it to Admiral Ohsugi. Since the captured Americans were naval aviators, Taniguchi also sent a copy to Admiral Furukawa at the nearby Kendari Naval Air Base.

The following day, a civilian interpreter named Ryuitsu Nose flew to Kendari with orders from Makassar to interrogate the prisoners. Nose had originally been sent out from Japan as a member of the Makassar Native Culture Research Institute, but by this

point in the war he had been pressed into service by the Japanese
Navy as a radio traffic monitor. He was fluent in English and had
graduated from the University of Southern California before the
war.

With Lieutenant Takita, Ensign Chiuma, an officer from the
23rd Naval Air Flotilla, and the interpreter Nose, Taniguchi went
through the interrogation of each prisoner again. He asked the
same questions in Japanese, through Nose, that he had asked the
prisoners in English the day before. Taniguchi confirmed that the
answers he heard this time were the same as those he received
when he talked directly to the Americans.

Although the prisoners told Taniguchi a number of things,
they were not completely honest. They said that this had been their
first combat mission and that they had just come from Australia.
The truth was that this had been their third armed Black Cat
mission, with dozens of other missions behind them, and that they
had been in the war zone for months. They probably lied about the
Gibson girl radio as well, making the Japanese think it was an
important piece of gear.

Two days after arriving in Kendari, the Americans were let out of
their cells and put to work maintaining the Tokkei Tai grounds.
The residents of Kendari saw them cutting grass, pulling weeds,
cleaning cars and trucks, and doing other manual labor.

Under their captors the nine young Americans faced a rough
and perilous existence. They surely expected to be killed soon after
being captured. But when they were interrogated by Taniguchi
and Nose, Taniguchi assured them that if they cooperated and
answered his questions, he would make sure they were sent on to
Makassar and a regular prisoner-of-war camp. Taniguchi told the
Allies after the war:

> On the night of the arrival of the prisoners of war, I
> met them. At that time I had a talk with the prisoners
> of war and I advised them and told them, "You are men
> who have surrendered," and I, as the commander of the

Kendari section, would accord them all courtesies due to prisoners of war, that being captured was nothing really to be ashamed of. I told them they would be questioned and I told them to tell truthfully and quickly everything that they knew and that I personally would see to it that they were sent to Makassar as quickly as possible since there were no quarters or compounds in Kendari where prisoners of war could be kept and that their presence would always be a worry to me. This was the first time that they smiled. They must have been thinking they were to be executed immediately, but my words seemed to have reassured them and that smile did give me the idea that my word had something to do with that smile. They said that they will do just as I say and asked me to assert my efforts to send them to Makassar. My English was not good, but seeing their faces, I thought I had Nose interpret for me and tell them what I had just said. Nose interpreted to them and they seemed to be quite reassured. . . . They began to drink coffee, smoke cigarettes and eat the fruits which we had given them. From that time on our conversations, which was rather informal, became smooth.

Though they had been assured they would not be killed outright, the men still had to survive the harsh treatment that the Japanese gave their captives all across the Pacific. Allied prisoners did not receive enough to eat and quickly lost weight. Medical treatment and supplies were lacking, and many prisoners died of dysentery, beriberi, pneumonia, and diphtheria. Some Allied prisoners in the Celebes were put to work in mines, where heavy labor and limited calories soon wore down their bodies. Although the nine Americans at Kendari did not have to do the backbreaking job of a miner, they were forced to work every day around the compound.

Three or four days after the initial questioning sessions conducted by Abe and Taniguchi, the Japanese began serious interro-

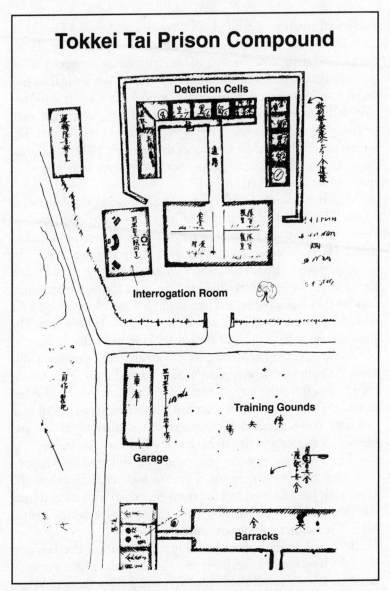

Tokkei Tai Prison Compound

Detention Cells

Interrogation Room

Training Gounds

Garage

Barracks

Drawn by an unknown Japanese artist for the trial of Gosuke Taniguchi.

gations of the nine captured PBY crewmen. Admiral Furukawa from the nearby naval airfield sent his chief of staff, Capt. Takao Sonokawa, along with another of his staff officers, to question the prisoners in detail through Nose. The Kendari Naval Air Base had an air intelligence section and could best extract relevant information from these new aviation prisoners. They questioned each prisoner separately in the interrogation room of the Tokkei Tai, with Taniguchi present for many of the sessions. What additional information the Japanese gained from this week-long round of questioning is unknown.

About two weeks later, they began questioning the Americans again. This time the naval staff officers from the airfield wanted the Americans to be brought to them, so they ordered Indonesian driver Harry Mesman to make a special trip to the airfield. His passengers were three of the Americans, including Joe Sommer and the lone surviving officer, Bill Goodwin. After tying the prisoners' hands behind their backs, and blindfolding them, two guards armed with rifles, bayonets affixed, accompanied them on their ride. The prisoners must have thought they were about to be killed.

Mesman drove his passengers to a small dwelling, about a mile from the airfield, that was being used as a guardhouse. Four Japanese officers from the airfield met the Americans there and questioned them again for more than two hours through an interpreter, probably Nose. After the interrogation the three were tied and blindfolded again and driven back to the Kendari Tokkei Tai.

The following day this procedure was followed by Mesman with the other six Americans. Three or four days after that, Bill Goodwin, Joe Sommer, and the third American with them during the first airfield interrogation were brought back to the guardhouse for another session with the Japanese.

It is not evident what additional information the Japanese thought they could learn from the nine airmen. The men could not have known much about what was going on in the war. When Captain Sonokawa reported to Admiral Furukawa on the interrogations, he told the admiral that after three days of questioning, he had learned nothing new from the Americans. At this point the interrogations of the nine Americans finally stopped.

The only real indication that the nine men were mistreated during all these heavy interrogation sessions was from one of the natives, probably Johan Tomasawa, interviewed after the war. He was also being held in the Tokkei Tai. Asked about what happened to the nine Americans during these interrogations, he replied, "They received beatings all over their bodies."

For Allied prisoners of the Japanese, physical abuse was commonplace. Although accurate details on the treatment of the nine Americans at Kendari are not available, guards typically were brutal to the prisoners under their control. Captives endured savagery from the lowest private to the highest-ranking officer and even from Japanese civilians working at the prison camps. Being beaten with clubs, sticks, whips, rifle butts, or wet ropes was a common occurrence for many prisoners.

During the next few weeks a routine developed for the prisoners at Kendari. The Japanese confined them in the Tokkei Tai at night but forced them to work around the compound during the day. The only difference since the interrogations had ended was that the Americans were now kept two or three to a cell. These cells were small and had no furniture, not even beds. According to the Japanese, each prisoner received a single blanket. Prisoners slept on top of their blankets since it was too hot to sleep under them.

During a questioning session with Allied investigators after the war, Captain Taniguchi said he had ordered that the prisoners be given mosquito netting and special foods since they "could not eat Japanese food." Tooru Tanaka, a chief petty officer at Kendari, said he brought canned milk, sugar, and other European foods from the airfield for the Americans. These Western foods, if they did exist, were probably supplies captured from the Dutch. But such kind treatment of prisoners is hard to believe since the Japanese universally fed their prisoners starvation diets and treated them like slaves.

While the nine Americans were enduring their ordeal in Kendari, the men of their squadron received the orders they had been anticipating. After more than three years in the Pacific and three combat tours, the squadron was heading home. On November 10, 1944, VPB-29 was officially relieved of combat duties by VPB-20. Some of VPB-29's planes were transferred over to other squadrons as replacement aircraft. Other PBYs loaded up with men from the squadron and took off, pointing their noses toward Hawaii. Their job was done.

The official squadron war diary shows the entire squadron in transit between November 12 and November 29. At the end of the month all the surviving members of the squadron were back on American soil, and the unit was disbanded.

Chapter 8

Shobun

The key to the fate of the nine American prisoners held in the Tokkei Tai prison compound was a radio message that Admiral Ohsugi, commander of the 23rd Special Naval Base Unit in Makassar, sent to Captain Taniguchi in late November 1944. Taniguchi understood this message as an order to kill the prisoners.

All written copies of the message in both Makassar and Kendari were destroyed by the Japanese near the end of the war. Ensign Dan, the Kendari communications officer who received the message, later reconstructed it from memory, and the note was translated into English from an official statement Dan made to investigators. The communication simply read: "Message Number XXXXX, should be executed or punished." "Message Number XXXXX" referred to the log number of a message that Taniguchi had sent to Admiral Ohsugi in Makassar on October 8, reporting the capture of the nine American airmen. The message's key Japanese word, or *kanji* characters, was *shobun*. Ensign Dan interpreted this to mean "execute the prisoners" who had been mentioned in the earlier message.

A few hours after Taniguchi received the *shobun* message, Captain Sonokawa called him from the naval air base to demand that four of the Americans be handed over. He intended to execute them at the airfield.

To Taniguchi, this was an order from a superior officer. Sonokawa was chief of staff to Admiral Furukawa, commander of the air base and tactical commander of the Kendari area. At 8:00 A.M. the next day, Taniguchi ordered that four of the nine Americans in the Tokkei Tai be delivered to units of the airfield to be executed.

This was not the only time during the war that one Japanese unit requested prisoners from another in order to kill them. Reports show that at a Japanese Army camp in New Guinea during 1944, a division commander obliged the request of a battalion commander by relinquishing two American prisoners. Both were put to death for the entertainment of the battalion commander and his troops.

The interpretation of *shobun* became critical to understanding the wishes of Japanese officers in Kendari and elsewhere during the war. Post-war testimony given by Japanese soldier Otogoro Ishida tells how the term was used in another case to call for the execution of American airmen.

Ishida's superior, Lt. Gen. Sanji Okido, developed a new policy on the handling of American prisoners. Japan was experiencing mass air raids by hundreds of B-29 bombers, and Allied airmen were being shot down over the Osaka area and captured in ever greater numbers during the last months of the war. Ishida told the war crimes court that Okido outlined the new policy to him early in June 1945.

> The commandant [Okido] suddenly called me to his office and expressed the following views:
> *a.* It appears that difficulty is being experienced because available facilities are too limited to cope with the sudden increase in the number of flight personnel held by the military police. In view of the fact that more and more increases must be expected we cannot allow the situation to stand. We must make some sort of disposition *(shochi)* immediately. Army headquarters are altogether too lax. They are virtually letting matters take their own course.

b. With the intensification of the air raids the people at large are suffering terribly and shrines and the Imperial Palace are being bombed. These flight personnel should be brought before military tribunals and severely dealt with *(shodan)* but nothing whatever has been done about them. The ones who are not needed here should be sent to PW internment camps but no such action has been taken. This is a serious problem. If they are going to leave the matter as it stands, no method of disposition *(shochi)* other than severe disposition *(shobun)* is feasible.

c. The commanders of all military police units will be given orders in keeping with the above and instructed to get in touch with and expedite the matter through the chiefs of the armies concerned.

Ishida apparently had no doubt about the meaning of *shobun.* He told the court that he immediately protested to Okido about this policy. He said he told his superior that:

The treatment of flight personnel, which is governed by international law, is the responsibility of the belligerent nations. Therefore as I have frequently explained before they should be handled with the utmost discretion and kindness. An illegal and unprincipled act such as severe disposition *(shobun)* must never be resorted to.

General Okido ignored Ishida's plea and even chastised him for his "routine approach" to the problem. As a direct result of Okido's new policy of *shobun,* captured American airmen were routinely executed by beheading, gunshot, and even poisoning. There was obviously no misunderstanding by those under Okido's command about the meaning of the term. Forty-five American airmen lost their lives because of Okido's new policy.

At the Kendari prison compound, Lieutenant Takita acted on Captain Taniguchi's order to select four of the Americans for execution. Takita randomly chose out Joe Sommer, Edwin McMaster, Walter Price, and Henry Zollinger. The date is believed to have been November 23, though some accounts differ.

Four junior officers from the units associated with the airfield came to the Tokkei Tai to pick up the doomed prisoners. Quietly overseeing the operation was Admiral Furukawa himself. Although he would later deny it, Furukawa followed the little convoy back to the airfield and witnessed each of the executions. Armed guards loaded the four prisoners into vehicles and rode with them toward the airfield.

Joe Sommer was the first to die. The small motorcade stopped between Kendari and the airfield at a village called Mondonga. Sommer was taken out while McMaster, Price, and Zollinger remained in their vehicles.

With only a few torpedoes to maintain and little else to do, Lt. Toshisuke Tanabe's aerial torpedo maintenance unit at Mondonga has been idle and bored. Officers and enlisted men from the unit, in full dress uniforms, were eagerly waiting for Sommer, and they cheered and clapped at the sight of their victim. Many in the crowd had obviously been drinking to celebrate the occasion.

A grave had already been dug by Indonesian workers brought from Kendari a little earlier, and a four-by-four stake had been driven into the ground at one end of the hole. Sommer was heard to cry out when he saw what awaited him. He was led to the grave site, where he was blindfolded and his hands were tied behind his back. He was forced to kneel in front of the hole and then tied to the stake, which came up to the middle of his back.

The officer selected as executioner raised his samurai sword and brought it powerfully down on Sommer's neck. The young American was beheaded amid great cheering and applause. Sommer's head fell into the grave. His body, with the stake still attached, was then kicked and pushed into the grave. The Indonesian workers were ordered to fill in the hole. As the Japanese dispersed, a number of them could be heard calling drunkenly for the other three Americans so that they could kill them too.

McMaster, Price, and Zollinger were still in their vehicles

about a hundred or a hundred and fifty feet away. They could hear all the commotion but could not see what was going on. But they did not need to see; they knew what had just happened.

After the execution of Joe Sommer, the motorcade left Mondonga and continued to the airfield. Whoever was organizing the executions had selected a site near some barracks, and the Indonesian grave diggers again went to work. The killing of the three remaining Americans was divided among the two antiaircraft units and the aircraft maintenance unit.

The order of the deaths of McMaster, Price, and Zollinger is uncertain, but each died as Joe Sommer had died. One of the three was led to a large grave and was beheaded by an officer of one of the airfield units. This unit left, and the men of the next Japanese unit came to await the next American. The second of the group was now brought to the site and beheaded. The last unit then executed the last of the three Americans in the same manner. Joe Sommer, Edwin McMaster, Walter Price, and Henry Zollinger were now dead and buried.

Back at Kendari the other Americans were being forced to work around the compound even as their comrades were being killed. The men did not have much longer to live, and they knew it. After the executions of the first four Americans, preparations got under way for the beheading of the remaining five.

These would be far more elaborate executions than those at the airfield. Captain Taniguchi gave the official responsibility for arranging these executions to Lieutenant Takita, his second in command. He told Takita to "abide by the samurai code" in killing the Americans.

Taniguchi announced at the officers' noon meal that the five prisoners would be executed later that day. It was November 24, though, again, some accounts differ. At about 4:00 that afternoon Takita sent for Ensign Chiuma. He asked Chiuma for the names of five junior officers, with the rank of warrant officer and above, who knew *kendo*, a combative fencing sport that used bamboo swords.

Chiuma named Lt. (jg) Toshio Mitani, Ensign Yoshitaka Ogawa, Ensign Isokichi Yamamoto, and himself. Takita wanted five executioners. He asked Chiuma if there was anyone else who might know *kendo*. Chiuma said that Tooru Tanaka, although not yet a warrant officer, was proficient in the sport. Takita then told Chiuma that Chiuma and the four he had named would be the executioners. He ordered Chiuma to tell them that the execution would take place in an hour.

Chiuma quickly informed the other designated executioners, changed into a dress uniform, and waited in his quarters. Mitani cleaned his sword and put on a dress uniform. Tanaka, being a noncommissioned officer, did not have a sword of his own, so he borrowed one from Torao Sato, the civilian police inspector. Ogawa and Yamamoto also prepared for the execution by putting on clean dress uniforms and waiting in their rooms until the appointed hour.

At about 5:00 P.M. each of them headed for the execution site independently. Chiuma, being in charge, arrived first, with the other four executioners arriving shortly thereafter. Between thirty and forty spectators came to watch the event.

The execution site was on a small plateau some forty feet up the side of a small hill, 160 yards or so in back of the Tokkei Tai compound. Some of the local Indonesians forced to work for the Japanese had already dug a large hole at the site. The hole was about twelve or thirteen feet long by five feet wide and five or six feet deep.

The prisoners arrived shortly after the Japanese. Bill Goodwin, Jake Nilva, Raymond Cart, Harvey Harbecke, and Paul Schilling—already blindfolded, hands tied behind their backs—were led from the prison compound to the execution site by Tokkei Tai guards.

No time was wasted. Bill Goodwin was forced to kneel by the hole while the other four were made to stand some twenty or twenty-five feet away. Chiuma ceremonially poured water over his sword blade, stepped to the left and slightly behind Goodwin, and raised his sword over his head with both hands. With the quick, strong stroke of a practiced samurai warrior, he cut off Goodwin's head. William Francis Goodwin, Jr., died instantly. The force of the blow to the back of his neck toppled his body into the grave. Chiuma then stepped back and cleaned the blood from his sword.

Chiuma called for the next American, who was led to a far end of the hole and forced to kneel. Then something strange happened. Instead of being killed next, the second American was left in the kneeling position while the third prisoner was brought forward and forced to kneel next to the spot where Goodwin had died. The second airman was to be executed by Tanaka, but after watching Goodwin die at the hands of Chiuma, Tanaka apparently became upset and nauseated. He had to turn his back and walk away from the executions for a few minutes.

Chiuma ordered Yamamoto to step forward. Yamamoto followed Chiuma's example and quickly beheaded the third American airman. The body toppled into the grave next to that of Goodwin.

As the second American still waited, kneeling, by the edge of the grave, Paul Schilling was brought forward and forced to kneel. Chiuma ordered Mitani to come to the hole. At Chiuma's command Mitani swung his sword down on Schilling's neck. (Paul Schilling was the only other victim besides Bill Goodwin who could be matched up with his actual executioner.)

It was now time to kill the second American, who had been forced to kneel at the hole while his friends were beheaded. Tanaka had regained his composure. At Chiuma's direction, Tanaka beheaded this man.

The last American was then led forward, forced to kneel, and beheaded by Ogawa. As with all the others, his body toppled into the grave from the force of the blow.

As the Japanese headed back to their barracks, the Indonesian laborers were ordered to fill in the grave and place a few stones around it as its only marker. All eleven crewmen from the ill-fated PBY that flew to Kendari on the night of October 1 were now dead.

Chapter 9

The Aftermath

As soon as the Pacific war came to an end in August 1945, Allied occupation forces moved into the Celebes Islands and other territory still held by the Japanese. Although the Dutch East Indies had been under colonial rule of the Netherlands before the war, it was the British who first moved into the many islands that now make up Indonesia. The Dutch were still recovering from the long war in Europe and German occupation, and they did not have the personnel needed to take back administration of the East Indies from the Japanese.

The conquering Allies quickly began investigating Japanese war crimes. Reports from soldiers who had served in the Dutch East Indies Army before the war and had survived the Japanese occupation were instrumental in starting a number of investigations. One report told of nine Americans executed at Kendari.

In early October 1945, Flight Lt. Martin O'Shea of the Royal Australian Air Force left Makassar for Kendari to investigate the report. O'Shea was among the Australian military personnel helping the British with their investigations. After a brief inquiry, O'Shea wrote a preliminary report dated October 19, 1945, that became known as "Australian Case No. 7, Beheading of Nine Americans at Kendari." The three-page document indicated that there had indeed been nine Allied servicemen, probably American, who had been held in Kendari and eventually beheaded.

O'Shea found some critically important inscriptions scratched into the walls of the cells of the Tokkei Tai prison. One inscription read:

> U.S.N.
> 2388974
> P. E. SCHILLING—CLINTON NEW YORK
> 10/44—11/44

Near that he found saw:

> U.S.N.
> J. J. SOMMER U.S.A.
> SHOT DOWN OCT. 1 '44
> BROUGHT HERE OCT. '44
> DEPARTED KILLED

And on another wall, he read an additional inscription:

> J. J. SOMMER
> 27 CONCORD AVENUE
> MAPLEWOOD
> NEW JERSEY

Both Paul Schilling and Joe Sommer knew that they were going to die and tried to leave some record of their presence. They were successful, and O'Shea reported their names to the Allied War Crimes Commission. O'Shea's initial report sparked further investigations. Soon members of the War Crimes Branch of the U.S. Army, now spread throughout Pacific, were dispatched to Kendari to dig deeper into Australian Case No. 7.

While the U.S. Army investigation team went to work in Kendari, O'Shea continued his own inquiry in Makassar. The British had set up large prisoner-of-war camps just outside Makassar, and almost all Japanese personnel from the Kendari area were held there. During December 1945 O'Shea started interviewing some of the Japanese from the Kendari naval garrison.

The Japanese civilian Torao Sato first revealed the story of the executed Americans to O'Shea. Sato was being held because of his association with the Tokkei Tai; he had been the police inspector attached to the Japanese Navy at Kendari. Sato was one of the spectators at the beheadings of the five airmen at Kendari behind the Tokkei Tai, and he had loaned his own sword to Tooru Tanaka for the executions.

From Sato, O'Shea learned the name of Captain Taniguchi and that Taniguchi had ordered the executions. Taniguchi was also being held at the prison camp, and O'Shea approached him with questions. Taniguchi readily admitted to ordering the execution of all nine Americans. But he said he did so under orders from his immediate superior, Admiral Ohsugi.

From Taniguchi and Sato, O'Shea acquired the names of the five Japanese who carried out the executions of the five airmen at the site behind the Tokkei Tai. He gave these names and the oral statement of Taniguchi to an American investigator, 1st Lt. Sheldon A. Key. Key compiled all the information and on February 26, 1946, submitted a new report on the atrocity at Kendari.

Armed with a growing list of Japanese suspected of being involved in the executions, an investigation team formally questioned the men in the prison camps. During April 1946 signed statements about the incident were taken from Sato, Taniguchi, and from four of the five known executioners: Toshio Mitani, Tooru Tanaka, Yoshitaka Ogawa, and Isokichi Yamamoto. Admiral Ohsugi was questioned and his statement was taken in May 1946 as he was being transported by ship from Makassar to Manila.

The investigators saw that there was sufficient evidence to bring charges of war crimes against all the Japanese involved, and they forwarded the reports, statements, and evidence to the Allied War Crimes Commission. The British transferred the Japanese prisoners to the Americans. Starting in October 1946, four trials would be conducted over the deaths of the nine airmen.

The name of another American airman was prominent in the
investigation of Kendari war crimes. Maj. John Z. Endress, commanding officer of the 339th Fighter Squadron, 13th Air Force,
was shot down by antiaircraft fire on January 12, 1945, while leading
a P-38 fighter sweep over the Kendari airfield. The 53rd Antiaircraft Unit stationed around the airfield, the same unit that
beheaded one of the PBY crew members, was credited with bring-
ing down the plane.

Endress survived his crash-landing and eluded the Japanese
for three or four days. But he had suffered head and chest injuries
and could not stay ahead of those hunting him. The Japanese
finally captured him while he was hiding in an abandoned hut, and
they took him to the hospital at the airfield. After some basic
medical treatment, Endress was transferred to the Kendari Tokkei
Tai, where he was imprisoned by the same Japanese who had held
the nine PBY airmen. Although severely wounded, he was interrogated by personnel from both the airfield and the Kendari
garrison. Captain Taniguchi, four officers from the airfield, and
interpreter Ryuitsu Nose all questioned the wounded major at the
same time. A captured enemy airman of such high rank was quite
an intelligence prize.

The Japanese were not known for their kindness to prisoners,
and in all probability Endress was beaten and tortured during these
interrogations. His "questioning" lasted five hours a day, every day,
for a week or more. He died a few weeks after his capture and was
buried near the common grave of the five PBY crewmen.

After the war the Japanese told investigators that Endress died
from wounds suffered when his plane crashed. But the American
investigator Key reached a different conclusion. In one of his written reports on the atrocities in Kendari, Key stated:

> He [Endress] sustained severe head and physical
> injuries and died after having been interrogated for five
> hours a day for six or ten days. It is believed that his death
> resulted from mistreatment in connection with this
> interrogation, particularly the forcing him to be inter-

rogated without giving him medical attention. . . . All during this time he was suffering from severe head injury. Upon his capture his injury was infected by flies. These Japanese [who testified after the war] did not state that they believe his death was due to the interrogation but all the evidence seems to point to that.

Unfortunately the War Crimes Commission did not think there was enough evidence to file charges. In a summary of crimes committed in Kendari, the Endress case was dropped with only a short comment:

All evidence points to the fact that he [Endress] died while in confinement in the Tokkei Tai detention cell at Kendari. There is no evidence that indicates definitely that he was a victim of an atrocity. It seems that he died of injuries received when he was shot down.

Nevertheless, the Japanese were charged in many other cases of reported war crimes. Subsequent trials fell into three groupings: Class A, B, and C. The Class A trial, conducted by the International Military Tribunal for the Far East, involved twenty-eight defendants who were the military and civilian leaders of Japan. These men were charged with plotting, starting, and waging the war. Their big, newsworthy trial, held in Tokyo between June 3, 1946, and January 24, 1947, was the equivalent of the Nuremberg Trials held in Germany after the war in Europe.

The Class A trial was an international effort. The judges, prosecutors, and defense lawyers were mainly civilians drawn from the eleven Allied nations who had fought and defeated Japan. All the accused were found guilty, and seven were sentenced to hang. On December 23, 1948, the seven were executed in Sugamo prison. The others served their prison terms in Sugamo prison until their parole in the mid-1950s.

The Class B and C trials were for specific war crimes in which actual incidents could be cited, with names of victims, dates, and places. Each Allied country conducted its own Class B and C trials. The United States held more than three hundred such trials involving at least thirteen hundred Japanese. The American war crimes trials were held throughout the Pacific, with most taking place in Guam, Manila, and Yokohama.

These trials were not conducted like typical American jury trials. Authority to hold the trials came directly from Gen. Douglas MacArthur as Supreme Commander for the Allied Powers. Each was conducted by a military tribunal or commission composed of three to five judges, one of whom, as "law judge" ruled on admissibility of evidence and testimony. The judges were almost always high-ranking officers and might be from any branch of the military services. Conviction under one of these tribunals required a two-thirds vote of the judges. Prosecutors and defense lawyers were usually American civilian attorneys supplied by the War Crimes Commission, although the accused could provide their own Japanese or American attorneys if they wished.

It was within this system that the Japanese from Kendari were brought to face justice. The American War Crimes Commission would take almost three years and four separate trials before ruling in the cases of all those involved in the killings of the nine Americans held in Kendari.

Chapter 10

The Trial of Admiral Ohsugi

The first officer to appear before a military tribunal in the deaths of the nine airmen was Vice Adm. Morikazu Ohsugi, the superior who was accused of ordering Taniguchi to execute the men.

Ohsugi was tried alone because the charges against him involved ordering the execution of four additional U.S. airmen some seven months after the Kendari killings. These four Americans survived the downing of a 13th Air Force B-24 bomber, a few miles north of Makasar on June 25, 1945, but were captured and beheaded in July at the military airfield outside Makassar.

In Manila on October 1, 1946—two years to the day after Jack Schenck's PBY took off on its last mission—the trial of the United States versus Morikazu Ohsugi began. He was charged, in general, with violating the laws and customs of war. The charges also said that he "wrongfully and unlawfully permitted and consented and/or ratified and failed to prevent and take corrective and punitive action against and/or failed to prevent and/or ordered and directed members of the Japanese Navy under his command to kill" thirteen then-unidentified American airmen.

Ohsugi pleaded not guilty. He maintained he knew nothing about the capture and execution of either group of Americans until after their deaths.

The first half of Ohsugi's trial concentrated on the Kendari executions. This part of the case hinged on the radio message that Ohsugi supposedly sent to Captain Taniguchi in late November 1944, ordering the executions. Ohsugi denied that any such message was sent. Unfortunately for him, the prosecution's first witness was Ensign Seijiro Dan, communications officer in charge of all radio traffic in and out of the garrison at Kendari.

Dan testified under oath that he remembered sending Taniguchi's original message reporting the capture of the nine prisoners to Ohsugi's headquarters in Makassar on October 8. The message was addressed to the commander of the 23rd Special Naval Base Unit, and Ohsugi was that commander. Dan also remembered receiving in late November a message addressed to Taniguchi from the commander of the 23rd Special Naval Base Unit. He testified that this message was in response to the October 8 note. Dan interpreted this second message, with its use of the word *shobun,* as an order to execute the prisoners.

Dan distinctly remembered taking this vital message directly to Lieutenant Takita, Taniguchi's executive officer. Takita, knowing the importance of the dispatch, immediately showed it to Taniguchi.

In defense, Ohsugi presented a statement that his Makassar communications officer, Wataru Yamasaki, made to Allied investigators in early 1946. Under pre-trial questioning by American officers and by Ohsugi himself, Yamasaki said he could not remember receiving or sending any messages concerning nine American prisoners at Kendari. (Yamasaki's questioning session was the only instance in which one of the accused was allowed to directly question a witness.) Yamasaki's written statement was in direct conflict with the testimony of Ensign Dan. But Yamasaki did not say that such messages were never sent—he said only that he could not *remember* any such messages.

Captain Taniguchi was the next prosecution witness. Taniguchi stated that he did not have authority to take action against the prisoners without orders from his superior, Admiral Ohsugi.

Taniguchi admitted that he had the Americans executed, but he said he did so because of the direct order he had received from Ohsugi—in the form of the *shobun* radio message.

Taniguchi also testified that in September 1945 he wrote to Ohsugi, asking why the American airmen were ordered to be executed. Taniguchi never received an answer. Some months later he met Ohsugi in a prison camp and again asked the same question. Ohsugi denied any knowledge of the executions.

Two of the executioners testified. Sazae Chiuma and Toshio Mitani described the executions in detail but could add little insight to the question of who actually ordered them. Chiuma did say that he had written a report about the capture and initial interrogation of the Americans, and that it was sent to Makassar a week or so after the prisoners arrived in Kendari. Chiuma had written the report at Taniguchi's request, and Taniguchi had sent it on to Makassar on the plane that took interpreter Ryuitsu Nose back to that city.

Throughout his trial Ohsugi continued to claim he knew nothing about the nine Americans in Kendari until long after they died. Although it would have no bearing on Ohsugi's trial, testimony in the subsequent Taniguchi trial seemed to disprove totally Ohsugi's pleas of ignorance and innocence. Sazae Chiuma stated under oath in the Taniguchi trial that he saw his own report at Ohsugi's headquarters in Makassar a couple of months later. Under questioning at Taniguchi's trial, Chiuma explained his encounter with his own written report:

Q: *Did you see any written reports concerning these American fliers when you arrived at Makassar?*

A: When the Americans arrived at Salabangka, I was to be in charge of the captured Americans, and to make a report to Captain Taniguchi. The report that I made to Captain Taniguchi was to be sent in turn from Taniguchi to Ohsugi. My report that was submitted to Taniguchi was submitted to Ohsugi with a few corrections, and that was the document that I saw at Makassar when I returned.

Q: *Can you explain to the Commission how you came to see
that report after you arrived in Makassar? Where did
you see it?*

A: At Makassar there is a General Affairs office, where
they handle such matters as personnel and reports. I
have a friend who works at that office, and he was
showing me some of the records. I noticed hand-
writing which was similar to mine, and upon closer
examination I noticed that it was a report that I had
previously submitted.

For some unknown reason this testimony was never brought out in
the Ohsugi trial.

Yet plenty of other evidence also indicated that Ohsugi knew
about the nine airmen from the beginning. After receiving
Taniguchi's message stating that some Americans had been shot
down a few miles north of Kendari, Ohsugi ordered that the floatplane be sent out to help in the search for the downed fliers. When
Taniguchi requested an English-speaking interpreter from
Makassar, Ohsugi ordered that Nose be sent over immediately.
When Taniguchi reported to Makassar that he had taken from the
Americans what he thought was an IFF electronic unit, Ohsugi
ordered that the unit be forwarded to Makassar. Furthermore,
Capt. Minoro Toyama, Ohsugi's second in command, admitted
that he knew about the nine Americans being held in Kendari. It
would have been strange for his boss not to know.

Although not mentioned during the trials, another incident
seems to indicate that Ohsugi knew about the captured Americans.
A few days after the nine airmen arrived in Kendari and the message of their capture was sent to Makassar, Tokyo Rose, Japan's
English-speaking radio propagandist, announced the capture of a
PBY crew in her broadcast to Allied forces in the Pacific. Taniguchi,
a naval captain commanding a small remote installation, would
not have been communicating directly with Tokyo, where Tokyo
Rose received her information. But Admiral Ohsugi was a high-
ranking flag officer, in command of a vast area of land and sea, and

he would have had direct access to the capital. He or his head-quarters staff must have notified Tokyo of the air crew's capture; This could not have been done without Ohsugi's orders or at least his knowledge.

The second part of Ohsugi's trial concentrated on the execution of the four American Army airmen in Makassar. The first witness in this part of the trial was Lt. Tokuji Shirato, who had been a legal adviser to the 23rd Special Naval Base Unit at Makassar. He testified that around the end of June 1945, Toyama asked him for an opinion on the legality of conducting a court-martial of the four captured airmen. Toyama was probably thinking about Japan's Enemy Airmen's Law when he asked this question.

Shirato studied the investigation and interrogation reports on the four airmen, then told Toyama that the airmen had not violated international law or rules of war and should not be court-martialed. Shirato testified that a few days later, Toyama again asked him whether he thought the Americans could be court-martialed, and he repeated his opinion for Ohsugi and Toyama. Shirato was sure Ohsugi heard the opinion, but the admiral made no comment.

Toyama then asked Shirato, "What shall we do?"

Shirato replied, "They should be put in the prisoner-of-war camp at Makassar or sent to Surabaja prisoner-of-war camp." Toyama said that they could do neither. The war was going badly for the Japanese, and these newly captured airmen knew it. Toyama did not want them combined with the other prisoners in Makassar. Most of them had been held since the early days of the war and were ignorant of the current situation; Toyama did not want them to learn that their side was winning. And the Japanese had no ships or planes left to send the four prisoners to Surabaja.

That afternoon, Shirato testified, he attended a staff meeting at Ohsugi's headquarters. Both Ohsugi and Toyama were present. At the end of the meeting, Lt. Comdr. Hikoichi Ishida, who reported directly to Toyama, announced that the four airmen would be executed the following day, July 8.

Shirato, stating that he was just a spectator, described the beheadings. The four prisoners were taken from the Judge Advocate building in Makassar and driven by truck to the outskirts of the Maros Naval Airfield. There Ishida took command of the execution party.

These executions were not as well organized as those that took place in and around Kendari seven months before. No grave was dug. Ishida selected the rim of a large bomb crater near the airfield as the site. The first blindfolded American airman was brought up and forced to kneel at the edge of the crater. At this point the "spectator" Shirato became involved in the executions: He had a list with the names of the condemned Americans, and as each was forced to kneel on the rim of the crater, Shirato asked the man's name and then checked it off his list. When asked by the prosecution to explain why he did this, Shirato answered "I had no special reasons for asking the names of these prisoners. I knew that this execution was wrong. There was a feeling of pity inside me and I thought that if I could take their names and pray for their memory, it would help."

After Shirato took the name of the first American, Ishida asked for a volunteer from among the spectators to behead him. No one stepped forward. So he ordered Lieutenant (jg) Inagaki to perform the first execution. The second American was then brought from the truck, and Ishida ordered Lt. (jg) Yoshiyuki Nakamura to execute him. Nakamura borrowed a sword from one of the officers in the crowd. Finally, Ishida ordered Lieutenant (jg) Nakao to execute the last two Americans.

Under cross-examination by the defense, Shirato brought forth the theory that Ishida had committed suicide after the war because he had been in charge of the executions and because he had been the officer in charge of the Makassar prisoner-of-war camp where, undoubtedly, other atrocities had been committed. He knew he would be tried as a war criminal and did not want to face it.

Shirato was not the best of witnesses. Long before the trial began, he had made his official written statements to investigators, but he kept volunteering new statements that contradicted earlier ones. The same thing happened during his testimony: The longer he spent on the witness stand, the more he changed his story. To some extent, the defense succeeded in discrediting Shirato, and the prosecution started to consider Shirato a hostile witness.

Also testifying in the trial was Lt. (jg) Goichi Saito, one of Ohsugi's minor staff officers. Saito had interrogated the four American airmen and had written the reports that Shirato used in his legal review. He testified that he had gone to the executions as a spectator with Shirato. He described the actual beheadings in far more detail than Shirato had.

About forty guards, spectators, and laborers were present during the executions, Saito testified. He said that Lieutenant Commander Ishida announced that the executions would now be carried out, by the order of a superior officer. With that, two guards brought the first blindfolded American from the truck to the edge of the crater and made him kneel. After receiving the verbal order from Ishida, Lieutenant Inagaki came forward and stood to the left of the kneeling airman. He raised his sword over his right shoulder, brought it down with a quick, strong stroke, and beheaded the man. The body, with the head still attached in front by a little bit of skin and muscle, fell over on its side. One of the guards then pushed it into the bomb crater.

The next two Americans were executed the same way, but trouble arose when the last American was brought to the crater. Ishida had ordered a fourth Japanese officer, whose name Saito could not remember, to behead him. After witnessing the three previous executions, this unnamed officer refused to do it. After much arguing and confusion, Ishida ordered Lieutenant Nakao, who had just executed the third prisoner, to finish the job. After the body of the last American was shoved into the crater, the work crew filled it in, and the executioners and spectators headed back to Makassar.

These two separate atrocities—the executions of the Naval PBY airmen in Kendari and the executions of the Army airmen in Makassar—were surprisingly similar. In both incidents the planes were hit by antiaircraft fire and crashed, with some crewmen surviving and evading capture for a few days. In both cases the Japanese officers who were sent to capture the downed airmen eventually took part in the executions. (Ensign Chiuma searched for the PBY crew near Salabangka; Inagaki and Ishida searched for the four B-24 crewmen and brought them to Makassar.)

Both sets of prisoners were turned over to the local Tokkei Tai for interrogation and holding. The naval captains involved with the two different incidents, Taniguchi and Toyama, were in charge of their respective Tokkei Tai units. In both incidents one of the actual executioners—Tanaka in Kendari and Nakamura in Makassar—had to borrow a sword from someone else in order to carry out his gruesome work. In both incidents, Ohsugi had allegedly ordered or permitted the executions, high-ranking officers directly under him had organized them, and junior officers had performed them.

On the afternoon of October 29, 1946, the trial of Admiral Ohsugi moved toward a close. All the evidence had been presented and the witnesses heard, and now it was time for the defense and prosecution to present final arguments.

The defense spoke first. Although the closing statement filled forty-six pages, it had little substance. Regarding the Kendari deaths, the defense counsel hinged his remarks on two main points. The first was that the prosecution had not proven, beyond a reasonable doubt, that the radio message ordering the executions was sent to Kendari. His second point, in apparent conflict with the first, was about the meaning of the Japanese word *shobun* in the message cited by Ensign Dan. The defense counsel argued that *shobun* had various meanings, such as "disposition, disposal, dealing, management, and punishment," as defined in Japanese-English dictionaries used by the court. He argued that Ensign Dan's testimony showed that the "punishment" meaning of *shobun* did not mean "to kill or execute."

The defense counsel also asked the judges to consider the conflicting and hostile interests of the witnesses against Ohsugi, most of whom were accused of war crimes themselves. This alone should raise a reasonable doubt as to the guilt of the defendant, he said, and necessitate a verdict of not guilty.

In his final statement the prosecutor rebutted the arguments of the defense and then summed up the case against Ohsugi. He addressed the court:

> From seeing his subordinates on the witness stand, it is obvious that Ohsugi ruled his command like a dictator. The Allied airmen and their constant bombing raids were making it tough for him. He became angered due to the destruction of his defenses. He decided upon retaliatory measures by killing captured airmen without authority from his superior. . . .
>
> Captain Taniguchi complied with his honor as a military man and declared the death of those airmen and stated that he never knew why the order was given to kill them. He requested Admiral Ohsugi to explain to this Allied Commission and the authorities since he himself could not give the explanation of that order and Admiral Ohsugi never had the courage to face reality and decided to let his subordinates take the blame. . . .
>
> Under command responsibility it is legitimate first in law and morals to comprehend . . . who, with the knowledge of an impending illegal act and with power, authority, and duty to prevent it, refuses to raise a hand in opposition. . . . Even if he knew of the impending commission of the illegal act or approved it after the deed was accomplished, he is guilty as a principal in that act. Such commanders who fail to prevent violations of war are themselves war criminals.

Ohsugi's trial ended on October 31, 1946, with a verdict of guilty on both charges of ordering and/or permitting the executions of the nine American airmen in Kendari and four in Makassar. He was sentenced to life imprisonment at hard labor. With completion of Ohsugi's trial, the stage was set for those of the other Japanese involved in the killings of the nine Americans in Kendari.

Chapter 11

The Trial of Captain Taniguchi

Next to stand trial in Manila were Captain Taniguchi and the four men under his command who were named as executioners in the killings of Bill Goodwin, Jake Nilva, Raymond Cart, Harvey Harbecke, and Paul Schilling.

Although the accused were charged with killing the five airmen, the prosecution did not yet have positive identification of the individual remains. Graves Registration had not completed official identification by the time the trial began, and the Americans' identities would not be confirmed until later.

Toshio Mitani, Yoshitaka Ogawa, Tooru Tanaka, and Isokichi Yamamoto were the executioners on trial with Taniguchi. One name was missing from the list: Sazae Chiuma. He would appear as a witness, but it had not been possible to bring him to Manila in time to be charged with the others. His turn would come later.

Chief prosecutor Thomas J. O'Connor, of New York City, traveled to Kendari before the trial to seek out additional evidence and witnesses. In October 1946 he led a small party of Americans from the War Crimes Commission to Makassar, where they became stranded because of the war for independence between the

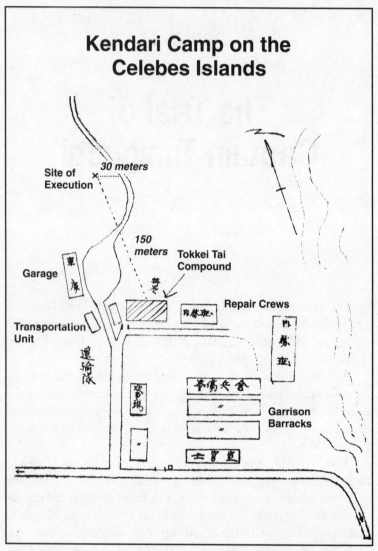

Kendari Camp on the Celebes Islands

This sketch shows the location of the prison compound and the site where American airmen Bill Goodwin, Harvey Harbecke, Raymond Cart, Paul Schilling, and Jake Nilva were executed. Drawn by Torao Sato for the trial of Gosuke Taniguchi.

Indonesians and their colonial Dutch rulers. At one point the American investigators had to fall to the floors of their hotel rooms as machine-gun and rifle fire flew in the streets outside.

After pressuring the Dutch, O'Connor finally got a military plane ride to Kendari. He had to go alone, however, leaving the rest of his party waiting in Makassar. He spent two to three weeks in Kendari, collecting evidence and interviewing native witnesses. By the time he returned to Manila, he was ready to go to trial, confident he had the evidence needed for conviction.

O'Connor's assistant for the trial was Thomas C. Fisher, of Louisville, Kentucky. One day as the two men worked on the case, O'Connor handed Fisher a list of the nine Americans believed to have been executed in Kendari. O'Connor then turned to work on some of his own papers. When O'Connor looked back, he saw Fisher gripping the list of names and crying. Fisher, it turned out, was a close friend of the Zollinger family and had known young Henry Zollinger for years. Fisher knew that Zollinger had been reported missing in action but, like the family, did not know his fate. The loss of Henry Zollinger was doubly tragic for his family, since Zollinger's older brother, a fighter pilot in Europe, had been shot down and killed a year before Henry was shot down in the Pacific.

On February 14, 1947, the trial was started in Manila. Taniguchi's defense was that he was following orders from a superior officer. The earlier trial of Taniguchi's superior, Admiral Ohsugi, had already established the fact of the *shobun* radio message, which was interpreted as an order to execute the Americans. A major portion of Taniguchi's trial centered around that message.

There was an odd twist to the proceedings. In Ohsugi's trial, prosecutors had tried to prove that the radio message from Ohsugi was the reason for the executions. But now, in Taniguchi's trial, prosecutors would try to prove that the message was *not* the reason for the executions—and that Taniguchi himself was responsible.

Controversy again revolved around the message's key Japanese character or word, *shobun*. As he did in the Ohsugi trial, Ensign

Dan interpreted the word for the court as "execute." Taniguchi's defense wanted to prove it meant exactly that, in order to convince the court that the message was Ohsugi's direct order to execute the airmen.

The prosecution countered with an expert witness. He was Richard M. Sakakita, a Japanese American who could read, write, and speak Japanese fluently. Sakakita, a member of the U.S. Army at the start of the war, had been taken prisoner during the Japanese invasion of the Philippines. He was forced to work as an interpreter in the Japanese Army legal section during most of the war.

The prosecution asked Sakakita to interpret the word. *Shobun*, he testified, meant "should be disposed of"; it did not mean "execute."

Under cross-examination by the defense, Sakakita was asked if he was familiar with the phraseology used by the Japanese Navy in radio messages. His answer was a straight "No, sir." The defense then asked him if *shobun* had any other meanings, and Sakakita stated that it also means "punishment" or "disposed of in the meaning of punishment."

It is interesting to note that Ensign Dan, who decoded the message, Lieutenant Takita, who physically delivered it to Taniguchi, and Taniguchi himself all interpreted the message as a direct order from Ohsugi to execute the airmen. They had no questions about the meaning of *shobun*.

The prosecution questioned Ohsugi directly about the *shobun* message during the Taniguchi trial. Ohsugi was shown Dan's reconstructed execution message:

Q: *I show you an answer on page 37 on an affidavit by Seijiro Dan, which is in Japanese characters, and ask you what does that mean?*

A: The meaning of this message is not clear.

Q: *Assuming that Taniguchi had received this "shobun" message, would you say, as an officer of thirty-six years experience, that there were any further steps he had to take. . . . What if anything should Taniguchi have done upon receipt of that message?*

The eleven American airmen who went down off the Celebes coast on the night of October 1, 1944, were flying a PBY-5 Catalina flying boat like the one pictured here. The PBYs notched a remarkable record in World War II for rescuing Allied military personnel from the ocean and for carrying out nighttime attacks against enemy shipping. *Courtesy of General Dynamics*

Bill Goodwin began to realize his boyhood dream of becoming a pilot when he was accepted in June 1942 as a Naval Aviation Cadet. *Courtesy of Goodwin family*

By the time Bill Goodwin left for overseas war duty in August 1943, he was engaged to Ginny Fleming. *Courtesy of Goodwin family*

(Far left) On May 28, 1943, William F. Goodwin, Jr., was commissioned an ensign in the U.S. Naval Reserve. *Courtesy of Goodwin family*

(Left) Jack Schenck commanded the PBY floating boat the night it went down. *Courtesy of Schenck family*

Arthur W. Kuhlman was also a pilot aboard the PBY. He was third in command after Jack Schenck and Bill Goodwin. *Courtesy of Kuhlman family*

The parents of Bill Goodwin were respected residents of Plymouth, Massachusetts. Bill Goodwin, Sr., was the city's postmaster, and Catherine (Clough) Goodwin was from a Plymouth family that traced its American history back to the late 1600s. *Courtesy of Goodwin family*

(Right) At six-foot-two, Paul Schilling was the tallest member of the PBY crew. He was the ordnance expert, manning the .30 caliber machine gun in the nose of the plane. *Courtesy of Goodwin family*

(Left) Harvey Harbecke, the senior enlisted man aboard the PBY, served as its plane captain, in charge of monitoring the engine's condition during missions. This country boy from Colorado joined the Navy in 1941 at the age of seventeen. *Courtesy of George Castille*

(Above) Henry Zollinger dropped his college studies of landscape architecture to join the Navy in July 1942. He was an extra crewman aboard the PBY the night it went down. *Courtesy of Zollinger family*

(Right) Walter Price *(top right)* posed for this photo with buddies from Navy Squadron VP-101 in May 1944. Price was another extra crewman on Schenck's ill-fated PBY. *Courtesy of Bud Smith*

Raymond Cart was a lookout aboard the PBY and manned a .50 caliber machine gun. At 120 pounds, this farm boy from Indiana was the smallest member of the crew. *Courtesy of Cart family*

Jake Nilva was the "old man" of the PBY crew; he was thirty-one when the plane went down. A lookout on the PBY, Nilva was in charge of a .50 caliber machine gun. *Courtesy of Nilva family*

Joe Sommer, a radio operator aboard the PBY flying boat, was an orphan who was raised by his aunt. *Courtesy of Bud Smith*

Edwin McMaster, a native of Chicago, was one of the two radio operators aboard the PBY. *Courtesy of Nilva family*

Jake Nilva *(top row, second from left)* posed with members of his plane crew before joining the crew commanded by Jack Schenck. *Courtesy of Nilva family*

Harvey Harbecke *(left)*, Walter Price, and two Australian girls had this picture taken at the beach during the period the American airmen were stationed in Australia. *Courtesy of Bud Smith*

Bill Goodwin met Valerie Storey—the girl who was to be his bride—in Australia in late 1943. *Courtesy of Goodwin family*

Bill Goodwin crouches on the wing of his PBY somewhere off the northwest coast of Australia in April 1944. *Courtesy of Goodwin family*

Valerie Storey in the car that Bill Goodwin ran on aviation fuel. *Courtesy of Goodwin family*

The crewmen of the PBY that Bill Goodwin flew with in April 1944 work on the plane off the northwest coast of Australia. *Courtesy of Goodwin family*

Arthur Kuhlman *(left)* is seen aboard a service boat taking him to his PBY aircraft. *Courtesy of Kuhlman family*

A crewman takes a dive off the wing of a PBY-5 assigned to Navy Squadron VP-101 in this 1944 photo. *Courtesy of Kuhlman family*

A group of Japanese military men stands on the dock at Kendari in the Celebes Islands to meet Allied representatives after the war. The nine American airmen who initially survived the downing of the PBY were held at Kendari. *Courtesy of Nilva family*

Japanese military men stand on the Kendari dock after their nation surrendered in World War II. The men had been assigned to military installations in the Celebes in what was then the Dutch East Indies. *Courtesy of Nilva family*

The nine American PBY crewmen were held in this Japanese prison compound, called the "Tokkei Tai," at Kendari in the Celebes. *Courtesy of Nilva family*

Catherine Goodwin prays at the grave of her son at the National Cemetery of the Pacific, Honolulu. *Courtesy of Goodwin family*

A: Taniguchi is a captain in the Navy, so granting that he received this message, he should have immediately contacted the issuer of that message in order to ascertain the meaning.

Much of the evidence against Taniguchi came from his own words. Taniguchi had made no less than four written statements to investigators about what happened to the nine American prisoners in Kendari and about his involvement in their deaths. During the war crimes investigations, written statements were taken from all the Japanese involved in the Kendari incident. Japanese interpreters were used even if the accused could speak English. After these sessions with investigators, the questions and answers were recorded, and each of the accused was given the chance to review and even revise his statement before signing it in front of witnesses. In his written statements Taniguchi repeatedly admitted that he ordered the execution of the five at Kendari and that he turned the other four over to the 23rd Naval Air Base for execution. He never once denied his involvement but stated repeatedly that he was "acting under orders." He made his most incriminating statement to investigators on April 11, 1946, at the Mandai prisoner-of-war camp near Makassar.

Q: *You say that these nine men were kept at the Tokkei Tai six or seven weeks. Then what happened?*

A: I received an order by radio about 23 November 1944 from Makassar to execute the nine American prisoners.

Q: *Who sent the message?*

A: Admiral Ohsugi.

Q: *Exactly what did the message say?*

A: I don't remember the exact words. It either said to dispose of or execute the prisoners and I am not sure which, but it was so worded that a possibility of mistake was very unlikely.

Q: *What action did you take upon receipt of this order?*

A: Lieutenant Takita brought the message to me and I

told him that we may as well go ahead with it. Takita said that he would make the arrangements and I told him that would be fine and that I would leave it up to him. Takita reported back to me that day and said that plans had been made to execute the prisoners the next day or two days later at about sunset. I approved of this plan and cautioned Takita to abide by the Samurai Code. About this time the Tokkei Tai received orders from the 23rd Air Unit at Kendari to send four of the prisoners to them. Takita brought the message to me. The order came from Commander Sonokawa. I saw no order. Takita told me about it and I don't know how the message was sent. Takita said that the 23rd Air Unit wanted to execute four. The orders from Admiral Ohsugi were to execute the nine prisoners so I didn't object to sending them, for all that I was interested in was that they be executed and the place and by whom was immaterial. I heard that a car was sent from the 23rd Air Unit to take the four back as it was about an hour drive.

Q: *What happened to the other five?*

A: They were executed either the next day or two days later as scheduled. I did not attend the execution but received the report from Takita. Takita did not attend the execution either but assigned Ensign Chiuma to do it.

Taniguchi's statement also mentioned that he had learned that the executioners were Sazae Chiuma, Toshio Mitani, Yoshitaka Ogawa, Tooru Tanaka, and Isokichi Yamamoto. Taniguchi's other statements, made both before and after this one, varied little in the circumstances of the executions. Taniguchi even took the stand in his own defense and told virtually the same story to the court.

During Taniguchi's time on the witness stand, the prosecution asked if he knew about the June 1944 order from the Imperial Japanese Navy that all captured Allied prisoners taken in his area be sent to the Surabaja prisoner-of-war camp on the island of Java. He said he did. Under questioning by the defense, Taniguchi again admitted he was aware of the order but said that he could not comply because of Allied air attacks and the resulting lack of transportation. But this defense strategy backfired badly as the prosecution went on the attack.

The prosecution called Harry Mesman, a former soldier in the Dutch East Indies Army who had worked for the Japanese in Kendari as a mechanic and driver. Mesman testified that during October and November 1944, the Kendari garrison had plenty of fuel, cars, trucks, and some motorboats.

Through cross-examining Taniguchi, the prosecution brought forth the fact that good, passable roads ran between Kendari and Kolaka on the west side of the peninsula between Bone and Makassar on the other side of Bone Bay. Taking prisoners to Makassar would have been a big step toward moving them to Surabaja.

The prosecution continued to discredit Taniguchi's testimony by causing him to admit that he regularly sent some of his own men to Makassar by this route during the latter part of 1944. The final blow came when Taniguchi admitted that two other American prisoners were transported from Kendari to Makassar by this very route in February 1945. Interestingly, the defense objected to almost every question the prosecution asked Taniguchi and Mesman about the transportation issue. But the court overruled almost every objection.

The four actual executioners who were tried with Taniguchi did not take the stand during the trial. Mitani, Ogawa, Tanaka, and Yamamoto—like Taniguchi—admitted their involvement but pleaded innocent because they were just "following orders."

Each of the four men made detailed written statements to war crimes investigators about their participation in the beheading of Goodwin, Nilva, Cart, Harbecke, and Schilling. These statements were used as evidence against them. The statement made by Toshio Mitani to investigators on April 12, 1946, was typical of those made by all the executioners.

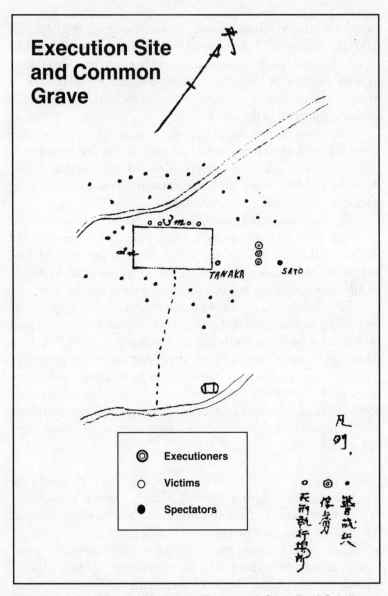

Bill Goodwin, Harvey Harbecke, Raymond Cart, Paul Schilling, and Jake Nilva were killed and buried here. Drawn by Torao Sato for the trial of Gosuke Taniguchi.

Q: *Who gave you the order to execute an American airman . . . ?*

A: Ensign Chiuma.

Q: *Why did you obey an order from Chiuma; wasn't he a member of the Tokkei Tai?*

A: I was convinced that the order came from Captain Taniguchi. I did not ask why I was the executioner because in the Japanese Navy we had to obey every order fully; I thought it over for a minute because the order had made me feel strange, then I told Chiuma that if it was an order I would obey it. Then he said it was an order, and to prepare immediately for the execution. This I did.

Q: *By "preparation" do you mean getting the sword and going to the place of execution?*

A: Yes. I had to clean my sword, put on a clean uniform, and go to the place of execution.

Q: *What time did you go to the place of execution that day?*

A: In the afternoon, about 5 o'clock.

Q: *Did you go alone?*

A: Yes, I went there alone.

Q: *Describe the execution place as it was when you arrived.*

A: When I arrived the five airmen, the other executioners, and about twenty or thirty guards were already there. This place was on a small hill about 150 meters from the garrison barracks.

Q: *Were there any spectators?*

A: There were about thirty men from Tokkei Tai and the garrison, and also one medical officer.

Q: *Was Captain Taniguchi there?*

A: No sir, he wasn't there.

Q: *Who was in charge of the execution?*

A: Ensign Chiuma.

Q: *Describe the Americans' position.*

A: The five airmen were standing about ten or fifteen meters from a large hole in the ground. They were blindfolded. I can't remember whether their hands were tied or not.

Q: *Can you describe their clothing?*

A: One of them, a lieutenant (jg) or first lieutenant, had on chocolate-brown overalls with a zipper down the front. Some of them wore dark blue pants and shirts with whitish lines running longitudinally through them. I don't remember their clothing very well.

Q: *Did any of the fliers wear any insignia?*

A: No, I don't remember any.

Q: *How did you know the one was an officer?*

A: Before, when the airmen were first captured, Chiuma told me.

Q: *Were the airmen led up one at a time to the hole to be executed?*

A: Yes, one at a time.

Q: *Then they were made to kneel in front of the hole, and executed with a sword, by severing or nearly severing the head from the body.*

A: Yes, exactly right.

Q: *Who killed the first American?*

A: Ensign Chiuma did. The first one was the officer.

Q: *Did the officer's body fall in the hole after Chiuma struck him with his sword?*

A: Yes, the body fell into the hole. I don't think the head was entirely cut off, but I think he died instantly.

Q: *Where were you standing at this time?*

A: I was about ten meters from the hole.

Q: *Who executed the next one?*

A: I don't remember.

Q: *Then who executed the third one?*

A: I executed either the third or fourth one. I don't remember which.

Q: *Who executed the last one?*

A: I think Tanaka did that one.

Q: *Who were the other executioners besides yourself?*

A: [At this point, Mitani named Chiuma, Yamamoto, Ogawa, and Tanaka.]

Q: *Did you see each of these four execute a flier?*

A: Yes, I saw each of the four men I just named execute one American each.

Q: *Who designated which one of the executioners would kill each airman?*

A: Ensign Chiuma.

Q: *Tell us about your part in the execution.*

A: After about three fliers had been executed, Chiuma told me to execute the next flier. Someone, I don't remember who, led the flier I was to execute to the hole and made the flier kneel in front of the hole. He was blindfolded, but I don't think his hands were tied behind him. Chiuma said, "Alright, now." I walked up to where he was and stood right behind him. Then I raised the sword up with both hands and struck the flier in the neck with 80 percent of my strength because, according to custom, the head should not be entirely cut from the body. Then blood spurted from the cut in his neck and he fell into the hole. I am sure he died instantly.

Q: *Did Ogawa, Yamamoto, Tanaka, and Chiuma execute their fliers in the same way?*

A: Yes.

Mitani left one detail out of his official statement: apparently he had once before beheaded someone. At some point late in the war crimes inquiries, an American investigator had asked some of the executioners of the Kendari five to reenact their parts in the killings for a photographer. The prosecution tried to enter these photos as evidence but eventually withdrew them after objections from the defense. On the back of one of these photos, Mitani had written in Japanese: "I am in the act of execution just as at Singkang."

Taniguchi's wife was present throughout the trial. Prosecutor O'Connor felt her presence was an attempt by the defense to influence the court. He explained his feelings in a letter to the Nilva family after the war:

They had Taniguchi's wife down from Tokyo as a
character witness, new Kimono every day. Someone
sold her a bill of goods, that underneath I was a kindly
gentleman and really felt sorry for her husband. The
day of summation she tried to grab my hands and kiss
them as I came into the courtroom. I dislike being rude
but I had to be.

On February 28, 1947, Taniguchi was found guilty of "wrongfully and unlawfully ordering the deaths of five Americans." He
was sentenced to be shot to death. A review board from the War
Crimes Commission later reduced the sentence to life in prison.

Mitani, Ogawa, Tanaka, and Yamamoto also were found
guilty and sentenced to prison for life. But within a few days, their
sentences—like Taniguchi's—were reduced by a review board.
Each of the four men would have to serve only ten years in prison
for taking the life of an innocent American.

Chapter 12

The Trial of Admiral Furukawa

The third of the four Kendari trials heard charges against Rear Adm. Tamotsu Furukawa and ten other defendants in the killings by the airfield. Furukawa commanded the 23rd Naval Air Flotilla (Kendari Naval Air Base) at the time of the executions of Joe Sommer, Edwin McMaster, Walter Price, and Henry Zollinger.

The trial of *The United States of America* v. *Furukawa* et al. began on May 24, 1948, in Yokohama, Japan. It would be the longest and most complex of the four trials, with the most defendants. The accused, along with Furukawa, were Capt. Gosuke Taniguchi, Capt. Takao Sonokawa, Ensign Sazae Chiuma, Capt. Yoshiotsu Moritama, Lt. Toshisuke Tanabe, Lt. Keiichi Nozaka, Lt. Yoshisa Nakata, Lt. (jg) Tokioka Maeda, and Ensign Katsuhito Imai. In his own trial, Taniguchi had already been found guilty of ordering the deaths of the other five American airmen. Although initially listed as one of the accused, Sazae Chiuma was dropped from this trial by the prosecution just as the proceedings began. He had been deeply involved with the five Kendari executions, but he had no part in the four killings at the airfield. He would stand alone before a tribunal after this trial was over.

As in the other trials, the written statements given by the accused during initial investigations were submitted as evidence. But unlike those presented in the other trials, some of these statements would prove to be grossly false. This trial would also involve, either through written statements or courtroom testimony, more evidence given by native Indonesian witnesses than in any of the other trials. This evidence would be the key to the prosecution's case.

Johan Tomasawa, an Indonesian soldier in the Dutch East Indies Army, was to be one of the most important and controversial witnesses in any of the trials. Tomasawa had been captured by the Japanese in January 1942 during the invasion of Kendari, held for three months, then freed when the Japanese Navy set up its administration of the Celebes. Shortly after his release, Tomasawa's house in Kendari was searched by the Japanese, who found a forbidden Dutch flag. Tomasawa was arrested, tried, and sentenced to twenty years at hard labor. He was serving this sentence at the Tokkei Tai prison compound when the nine American airmen were brought in.

Tomasawa was forced to do general work around the Tokkei Tai, cutting grass, pulling weeds, doing laundry, cooking, and washing dishes. He had one additional duty: digging graves for the victims of the Japanese. He did not work alone at this gruesome task; eleven other Indonesians who had also been taken prisoner on the day Kendari was invaded were forced to dig graves with him.

Prosecutors flew Tomasawa in from Indonesia as their star witness, and one of his first remarks threw the courtroom into chaos. He was asked by one of the prosecutors, "Where are these other eleven?" His quick answer, made through an interpreter, was, "They were all beheaded."

The defense attorney jumped from his seat and loudly demanded that the court declare a mistrial on grounds the prosecution was eliciting "information from the witness not relative to the issues in this case, but which reflects against the accused." He went on with his passionate plea to the court: "I have never seen a case where evidence of outside atrocities was ever brought into a courtroom deliberately, apparently, as in the questioning of this witness. . . .

I submit that questions are deliberately posed to the witness, the sole purpose of which can do nothing more than create prejudice."

The prosecutor was surprised by Tomasawa's answer and the defense's quick reaction to it, and he took a second or two to respond. He told the court that Tomasawa's answer was unexpected; he had expected to hear only that the eleven were dead. He claimed that he pursued this line of questioning only to show why he could not produce other witnesses.

The judges called a recess to discuss in private the defense's motion for mistrial. Twenty minutes later the court reconvened. There would be no mistrial, the court president said, but the question and Tomasawa's controversial answer to it would be struck from the record.

Tomasawa said that he worked with the American prisoners, doing jobs around the Tokkei Tai. But he did not talk to them, he said, because he could not speak English. Tomasawa then testified about the day the four Americans were executed.

Tomasawa said that he and the other Indonesian workers, along with Japanese guards, were taken to Mondonga in a bus or truck driven by Harry Mesman, while the Americans rode in cars driven by the Japanese. At the site the Indonesians were told to dig a hole. Tomasawa recounted the details of Joe Sommer's execution, the first of the four:

Q: *Now, after you dug the hole, what happened, if anything?*
A: After we finished with the hole, the motor cars carrying the Americans arrived, whereafter one of the Americans was taken out blindfolded and his hands tied and led to the hole.
Q: *After reaching the hole, what if anything happened?*
A: After reaching the hole the American was made to kneel down and was beheaded.
Q: *I will ask you to state whether or not you saw a stake driven near the hole.*
A: Yes, there was a pole near the hole to which the American was tied up.

Q: *Was the American tied to the stake in a kneeling or standing position?*

A: [Tomasawa did not answer verbally, but left his chair, kneeled, and held his hands behind him near his buttocks with his head leaning forward.]

Q: *Was the body released from the pole before being pushed into the hole?*

A: The body was not untied, but it was pushed into the hole together with the pole.

Q: *After that, I will ask you to state whether or not you and your companions filled in the grave.*

A: We filled the grave.

Tomasawa was asked if he could recognize any of the defendants as being at this execution, and in reply, he pointed to Taniguchi, Imai, and Maeda. Tomasawa said that although he could not point him out in the courtroom, Admiral Furukawa was also at the Mondonga execution.

The prosecution asked Tomasawa why he thought Furukawa was present if he could not identify him in court. Tomasawa answered that he saw a staff car flying a small yellow flag, an indication that an admiral was riding inside. Furukawa was the only admiral in the area.

Investigators asked Captain Sonokawa about these small flags about two months before the trial, and this information was included in his written statement.

Q: *Did any of these staff cars besides Furukawa's have a pennant or any distinguishing flag?*

A: Yes, they did. Japanese Navy regulations prescribed that admirals' cars would fly a yellow flag; captains, commanders, and lieutenant commanders a red flag; and below that a blue flag. These regulations were very strictly adhered to.

Q: *You said that the flags were never flown unless an officer of the proper rank was in the car. Did an officer ever ride without the flag?*

A: No, that would never happen. If an officer is in the
car, the proper flag is always flown.

Tomasawa then told the court what happened at the airfield.
He and the other Indonesians were ordered to dig a larger hole than
that at Mondonga. About half an hour later, three cars arrived with
McMaster, Price, and Zollinger. They were taken out one at a time,
tied to poles driven into the edge of the hole, and beheaded. About
half an hour passed between each execution.

At this point in the trial some confusion developed over
Tomasawa's testimony. He said that all three Americans were executed at the same spot and buried in the same hole. But the Japanese who were involved with the executions testified in their written
statements that the Americans were executed separately and
buried in individual graves.

Tomasawa had some difficulty explaining through the interpreters that there was no real discrepancy. He and his companions
had dug a long hole, and after each execution they filled it enough
to cover the body while the Japanese who killed the man left the
area. Soon the next group of Japanese arrived and executed the
next American, and his body was also covered with dirt. And so it
went with the other two executions. To each group of Japanese it
looked as if only a single prisoner were being executed at that spot.

After the prosecution questioned Tomasawa, the defense team
took their turn. Their tactic was to discredit Tomasawa and his
testimony by asking him a question and then asking a similar question later, hoping for a different response. The defense counsel appeared to be successful in a few such instances. For example,
Tomasawa was asked if his family lived with him in Kendari. He
said no. The next day the defense asked him, "Where did your
wife live during the year 1944?" He answered, "In Kendari." The
defense counsel quickly pointed out to the court the difference
between this answer and Tomasawa's reply from the previous day.
But to Tomasawa there was no discrepancy: In his culture, "family"
meant parents, brothers, sisters, and grandparents, not just a spouse.
His wife had been with him in Kendari, but his family had not.

After several seemingly conflicting answers from Tomasawa,

the defense counsel accused him of lying to the court and even claimed that he had "absolute evidence" of Tomasawa's falsehoods. The counsel demanded that Tomasawa be reminded that he was under oath and that he could be punished for lying. Tomasawa was so reminded by the court. The defense counsel then continued his questioning without revealing his "absolute evidence." In only a few instances could the defense cause Tomasawa to admit he changed his story on some minor fact, and when this happened, Tomasawa simply stated that he was confused by the number of questions thrown at him and by the long time between the incident and the trial—almost four years.

It was difficult to convey the questions and answers. Tomasawa, an Indonesian, spoke only Malay, so all the questions and answers went through two interpreters. While Tomasawa was on the witness stand, an Indonesian interpreter would translate from Malay to Dutch, and a Dutch interpreter would translate the Dutch into English. Language differences caused many difficulties: Malay has no singular or plural forms, and in Malay the same word can mean both admiral and general. Many times Tomasawa was accused of giving false testimony or changing his story when the discrepancy was nothing more than a mistranslation of his answer.

Trial transcripts reveal the tension between Tomasawa and the defense counsel during the two and a half days the defense questioned him. Tomasawa handled himself well under the steady pressure, and even through two interpreters he was able to get in a shot at the defense counsel. Asked if he really expected the court to believe his answer to some minor question, Tomasawa replied, "If that is not believed then what is the point in my having made oath?" The counsel ignored this response, dropped the subject, and quickly turned the questioning in another direction. Though the defense worked hard to challenge Tomasawa's testimony about Admiral Furukawa, Tomasawa continued to insist that he saw Furukawa's car at both execution sites.

At one point during Tomasawa's long testimony, he related the strangest story about Kendari. Several months after the nine U.S. airmen were executed, a fisherman named Badaeng found a woman

floating in a life raft off Wowoni, a large island a few miles southeast of Kendari. The fisherman took her and the raft to Kendari
and gave them to the Japanese, while Tomasawa watched them
arrive.

Tomasawa thought the woman was Dutch, but he soon was
told by a friend who spoke English that she was American, although
her identity was never proved. She was about 5 feet 6 inches tall,
and had very light skin, blond hair, and blue eyes. She was wearing
a khaki uniform with slacks, and she seemed to Tomasawa to be in
good physical condition. Where she was from and how she came
to be on a raft were never determined.

The Japanese placed the woman in a house they used as temporary quarters for officers traveling through Kendari. They did not
guard her; she was simply told to stay in the house, and she did.
The Japanese put her to work sewing and repairing their uniforms.

Four or five days after she was brought into Kendari, Tomasawa
related, the woman was taken from the house and driven to Mondonga. Tomasawa was ordered to dig a grave, and when it was
finished, he stepped back and witnessed the woman's execution.
During the Furukawa trial he described the beheading.

Q: *Do you know how she was executed?*
A: That woman was tied to a small tree, as small as this
here. [At this point, Tomasawa pointed to the micro-
phone stand, which was about three-quarters of an
inch in diameter.] It is a kind of fruit tree. It was a
young nanka tree as big as this. . . .
Q: *Was she in the standing position that you just indicated,
or was she kneeling?*
A: No, she was standing and the nanka was tied to her
body with a rope. . . . The nanka tree was curved and
it followed the curve of her body in the position she
was standing in. It followed the curve of her body
and she was tied to the tree in that position.
Q: *Was she or was she not blindfolded?*
A: She was blindfolded.

Q: *Where were you when this woman was executed?*

A: I was at that time right there because I and my companions were made to dig the hole and after we finished digging the hole we stood about ten meters distance from the grave.

Q: *I will ask you to state whether or not you and your companions filled the grave after the execution.*

A: Yes, we did fill the grave.

Q: *Do you know who actually wielded the sword that beheaded this woman?*

A: One Japanese from the Tokkei Tai called Abe.

Q: *Was that the Tokkei Tai whose headquarters was in Kendari?*

A: Yes, it was.

Q: *Now, explain to this Commission how Abe beheaded this woman, being tied to this small sapling or tree.*

A: She was being tied to this young sapling which bent through the woman's weight. She was tied with—she was tied at the shoulders and she bent forward and the tree bent along with her. At that time when she was standing in this position she shouted something, what I did not understand. Then a Japanese came forward and removed the blindfold and when she was about to be beheaded she said something like "Mother, Mother!" So she was—so when she was beheaded she didn't have the blindfold on.

Q: *Now, was this young tree growing at that place or was it just the trunk of the tree driven into the ground?*

A: That sapling was there already—was growing there.

Q: *Now, I will ask you to state whether or not the body was loosened from the tree in any way or how it was put into the grave?*

A: The body was—the rope tying the body to the sapling was cut off and only the body was pushed into the hole, but the part of the sapling that was cut off together with the head went also into the hole with the head.

Abe, the woman's executioner, was the chief warrant officer from the Tokkei Tai. His name appeared repeatedly in investigation reports and court records, as his involvement with the many deaths in Kendari started early and continued to the end of the war.

His name first appeared in connection with the June 1942 executions at Amoito, near Kendari, of the British merchant ship's crew. Not much attention was paid to Abe in the war crimes investigations because he killed himself shortly after Japan surrendered. He must have feared what would happen to him when the Allies arrived.

The Japanese in Kendari knew that their crimes would be investigated and punished. Those involved with the deaths of the nine airmen admitted to long conversations about that possibility before the Allied troops moved in. Abe may have thought that the Allies would hang him. As the individual who actually ran the Tokkei Tai, he was probably involved with most of the beating, torture, and killing that took place there. Commissioned officers were transferred in and out of Kendari throughout the war, but Abe was there the entire time.

The testimony of Johan Tomasawa, the prosecution's star witness, ended with a bizarre twist: he never completed it. During cross-examination by the defense, Tomasawa revealed that during the war he had made some personal notes about the executions. He left them in Indonesia in his foot locker, he said. Both the prosecution and the defense wanted to see the notes, and the prosecution even suggested that the court reconvene in Kendari to look at the site of the executions and to try to discover more evidence.

Although the court declined to go to Kendari, it gave permission for the prosecution and defense attorneys to travel there. At the same time, Tomasawa was directed to return home for his notes and to return to Yokohama with them. The court adjourned on June 7, 1948.

When the group from the trial reached Makassar, Tomasawa was sent on to Batavia, Java, to find his notes. He later dispatched a telegram to say that he would be delayed in returning. And that was the last he was heard from.

Tomasawa's fate remains unknown. He might have become involved in the armed revolt of the Indonesian people against Dutch colonial rule. As a soldier in the Dutch East Indies Army, he may have been forced to return to active military service. He could have joined the resistance and fought for independence. He may have simply decided he did not want to endure any more of the verbal abuse being handed out to him by the defense in the trial. Perhaps Tomasawa lied about having notes at home to allow him to leave Japan and return to Indonesia. In any case, Tomasawa did not return, and the trial went on without him.

Captain Taniguchi stood in his own defense. He repeated his story about receiving the *shobun* execution message from Admiral Ohsugi and his testimony about receiving a request from the Kendari Naval Air Base, Furukawa's command, to send four of the Americans to the airfield for execution. He brought forth nothing new.

Of the remaining defendants, only Katsuhito Imai took the stand. He told the court that he was ordered by one of the other defendants, Toshisuke Tanabe, to go to Kendari to pick up one of the Americans. Tanabe's written statement about Joe Sommer's execution claimed that he had been shot by a firing squad, not beheaded. Imai also told the court that the prisoner was shot by a firing squad. His testimony differed from Tanabe's written statement in that Imai said an officer named Okitsu ordered the squad to fire, whereas Tanabe stated that he had personally given the order.

Imai and Tanabe both lied about the form of execution. It seems as though the two had collaborated before the trial, but Imai could not keep his story straight. Unfortunately, the truth about how Joe Sommer died would not come out in this trial.

Johan Tomasawa's earlier testimony contradicted both Tanabe's written statement and Imai's testimony: Tomasawa insisted that Sommer was beheaded, not shot. The defense had tried to get Tomasawa to change his story, but Tomasawa would not relent.

The subject was never fully resolved during Furukawa's trial. A report that would have resolved the question was buried in the records of the subsequent trial of Sazae Chiuma. This report, the medical record on the remains of Joe Sommer, had been forwarded to the War Crimes Commission too late to be used in the Furukawa trial. It really had no bearing on the case against Chiuma, who was not charged in Sommer's death. Made out by an Australian Army doctor attached to the graves registration team, the report stated that the individual, who later proved to be Joe Sommer, was beheaded.

> I have examined the bones exhumed by the previous witness in this bamboo grove about a mile from the village of Diji [near Mondonga]. They are the bones of a male body, which had short hair, dark-brown rather than black. The body was beheaded with a sword or ax, more probably a sword. He was struck by a right-handed man from above and behind. The victim was in a crouching or kneeling position with the head bowed. Multiple blows were struck from the back. There were two blows across the back of the neck, severing the seventh cervical vertebrae. There was one blow across the right cheek, severing the right ascending ramus of the mandible. Another blow severed obliquely the left clavicle. The blows would be delivered downwards by a right-handed man. The first rib also was severed. I have also examined the crosses located in another grave. From the posture, it is possible that the victim could have been tied to such a cross. It is difficult to say with any degree of exactitude. With the bones, on the body, were American trousers with American buttons; presumably an American airman. He was about 5 ft 10 ins in height. Age between 20 and 30.

In other words, Joe Sommer was not shot by a formal military firing squad—he was hacked to death. His executioner hit him with a sword around his head and shoulders four or five times before he finally died.

This account was substantiated by a witness to the execution, Harry Mesman, the local man who worked as a driver and mechanic for the Japanese. Mesman had driven one of the vehicles that day, but he was ordered to leave the area during the execution and stay in his nearby house. From a hidden spot in the house, Mesman watched the beheading. He described it to investigators on November 21, 1946.

> A Japanese officer stepped up with a sword and struck the American on the back of the neck. I closed my eyes. I could hear a scream or loud groan as the blade struck—then all the Japanese cheered and yelled. A Jap soldier came to my house and told me to come out and get on the bus (truck). The Japanese came around the truck, cheering and jeering—some seemed to have been drinking—I heard one say "Why can't we keep the other three and kill them here?" An officer ordered the bus to proceed to the guardhouse at the airfield. There the other three Americans were taken out of the bus. It was the last I saw of them. I was told to go back to Kendari. One of the Jap guards told me that the three were to be killed by different units at the airfield.

A man whose head is quickly severed from his body cannot scream as Joe Sommer did. Empirical evidence shows that Sommer was beaten just before he died; the dental chart used by Graves Registration to identify Sommer's remains shows that four of his top front teeth and six of his lower front teeth were missing. From the dental chart it looked as though they had been knocked out of his mouth by what might have been a boot or rifle butt.

When an adult's tooth is pulled or knocked out, the jaw bone starts to grow rapidly to fill in the hole left by the missing tooth. This growth starts within a week or so, and a forensic specialist can tell from the amount of bone growth around a missing tooth's socket approximately how long before death the tooth was lost. If a tooth is lost at the time of death or after death, the jaw shows no bone growth.

Sommer's skull showed no such bone growth, and on the chart all ten missing teeth were marked as being lost posthumously. But they were more likely knocked out just before he died. Buried immediately after death, Sommer's body was not disturbed until the Graves Registration team exhumed it. Of the dental identification charts made of the six bodies that were recovered, only Sommer's reported the loss of teeth posthumously.

The beating was substantiated by Harry Mesman in a different statement made to investigators in March 1947:

Q: *On the day these first four were executed at two different points, were they mistreated in any way?*
A: Yes, they were beaten. I saw it.

The trial of Furukawa and the others concluded in mid-July 1948. For Captain Taniguchi, the defense had entered a late plea of double jeopardy because he had already been convicted on similar charges in the earlier trial. The court sustained the plea and found him not guilty in this trial.

Sonokawa and Imai were acquitted. Of all those accused in the killings of the nine Americans, these two were the only ones found not guilty. Sonokawa had produced evidence that he had been in Surabaja when the executions took place, and the court felt that none of the evidence showed that Imai was involved in the actual executions. His only part in the events was that he followed orders to pick up one of the Americans from Kendari. Had the court learned of his lie about the manner of Joe Sommer's execution, the verdict for Imai might have been different.

The other seven defendants were found guilty, with each receiving a seven-year sentence. At the time of sentencing, all except Keiichi Nozaka petitioned the court for clemency. The petitions, written in Japanese and translated for the court, stated that the guilty were good men who had families that would have no one to support them if the men went to prison. Some of the petitions went so far as to point out that a few of those convicted were "good Christians."

The petition for Yoshisa Nakata had more than 21,000 signatures; the one for Yoshiotsu Moritama had more than 47,000. But the court was not impressed. The only mercy shown the guilty was the reduction of one month off their sentences for time already served. Even Nozaka, who had not submitted a clemency petition, received this reduction.

Some months after Furukawa's trial, the mandatory review board upheld the conviction of Admiral Furukawa. The board's written summary stated that the "distribution of the four POWs to the various units [under Furukawa's command] was in the nature of staging a Roman Holiday and a morale builder." The summary later went on with more descriptions of the circuslike atmosphere of the executions:

> Each of the accused in the case at bar was an officer in the Japanese Navy. It cannot be said that they were ignorant and trusting members of a firing squad who are marched in squad formation to the scene, ordered in a group as part of military routine, deliver their fire and are marched away. These accused persons presumably of training and intelligence, are men who could, and without doubt did, observe the manifest pointers which marked these killings as capricious and illegal morale builders. The scene at Mondonga is illustrative. Personnel were called out in their dress uniforms and attended the tragi-gala scene with cheers, applause, and drinking. This is not the setting of a solemn military execution under legal orders.

The War Crimes Commission reported it was obvious that the four airmen executed around the airfield were killed in an effort to raise the morale of the Japanese troops. It is likely that the five others at Kendari died for the same reason.

When asked why the Americans were killed, Furukawa answered: "It is just my opinion, but I think the fliers were killed because of the antagonism of the Japanese people towards American fliers. When any were captured, that was the first thing they thought of."

Chapter 13

The Trial of Ensign Chiuma

The man who beheaded Lt. (jg) Bill Goodwin was the last to stand trial. Sazae Chiuma faced the court in Yokohama in what was the shortest of all of the three hundred American-held war crimes trials against the Japanese. Chiuma's trial lasted less than one hour in total: fifty-two minutes on July 29, 1948, and five minutes to conclude it the following day.

Chiuma's defense consisted of a court-appointed American attorney and a Japanese attorney whom he had chosen. There is no evidence, however, that his hand-picked attorney actively participated in the defense. Chiuma faced two charges: executing Bill Goodwin and directing Mitani, Yamamoto, Ogawa, and Tanaka to kill the other four Americans at Kendari. He pleaded guilty to the first charge and not guilty to the second.

The only evidence the prosecution submitted was written reports and statements, such as the Graves Registration reports on the recovery of the remains of the five killed at Kendari. They also introduced Chiuma's official statement and the written statements of Admiral Ohsugi, Captain Taniguchi, Ensign Dan, Mitani, Yamamoto, Ogawa, and Tanaka. These statements had all been previously used in the trials of Ohsugi, Taniguchi, and Furukawa.

Chiuma took the stand briefly to identify himself to the court and to state that he understood the charges against him. Instead of giving new oral testimony, he relied on his written statement made to investigators on August 12, 1946. In it he described his version of the executions, including his claim that an individual he identifed as Ensign Kakita was in charge.

Q: *Describe in detail the manner in which each American was executed.*
A: The grave was a rectangular one. The people were in back of the grave and surrounded three of the four sides. One side was open and the five Americans were about ten meters in front of the open side of the grave. The Americans were blindfolded and their hands were tied in front of them. The Americans were stationed in front of the long side of the grave. On the opposite long side Kakita was at one end. I was directly in back of Kakita. One of the Americans was brought up to the base, or short end of the rectangular grave, by a guard. Kakita and I were at the other far corner end of the grave. The American was made to kneel, with his hands on his knees, and bending over the grave. Kakita then turned to me and said that I should execute the American. I took my sword out, put some water on it, walked from Kakita around the grave to where I was standing at the left side of the American, and took a position with my feet slightly apart. I raised my sword with both hands high above my head, grasping the handle firmly. I then brought the sword down with a swift sharp stroke. I was excited and confused and do not remember all of the details clearly. The American toppled into the grave immediately after I had executed him. I cannot say whether his head was completely severed but I know that he lay in the grave and did not move. After executing the first American I walked back

around the grave at the rear of Kakita and there cleaned my sword. I then stayed near Tanaka and Yamamoto while each of them took one of the four Americans who were brought up to the same place, where I executed the first American, and there the same thing was repeated. I actually saw Mitani, Ogawa, Yamamoto, and Tanaka each execute an American. After the fifth execution the guards and soldiers filled in the grave in which the bodies were lying. And I saw each American's body topple into the grave. After this we all made a prayer for the departed soldiers.

Q: *What happened next?*

A: After the grave had been completely filled in we all left for our respective quarters. I do not remember too well what was said and done because I was still very excited and confused.

Q: *Were you in charge of the execution?*

A: No. Kakita was in charge and gave the orders to each one of us for the execution.

Chiuma was not questioned or cross-examined by either the prosecution or the defense at his own trial. During the earlier Taniguchi trial, however, Chiuma had spent a great deal of time on the witness stand. As in his written statement, he had tried to convince everyone that he was not the one in charge of the executions.

Q: *Did you have charge of the execution of these prisoners of war?*

A: No, it was Ensign Kakita. . . . Before the execution, Kakita guarded the five American prisoners and told them that up to now he was treating them as American heroes, but pursuant to orders, they had to be executed. Before the execution, he told me that he had been ordered to take charge of the actual execution, but that there were no orders as to who would actually perform the execution. He was my superior, so it was not possible that I would be the one in charge. He ordered me to execute the first prisoner. Then he said, "Next." Nobody volunteered, so I followed him, and ordered Tanaka, Mitani, Yamamoto, and Ogawa to perform the executions in that order. Because I was the one who gave those names, due to the fact there were no volunteers, it seemed I was the one in charge and that is a mistake.

Chiuma's attempt at placing the blame on Kakita did not work. Everyone else associated with the execution of the five in Kendari stated that Chiuma was in charge. Taniguchi stated that the commander of the Tokkei Tai had "assigned Ensign Chiuma to do it." Ensign Kakita was never questioned or charged with any crime. He may have been present at the executions, but only as a spectator. Even Sato, the civilian police inspector who witnessed the five Kendari executions, said that Chiuma was in complete charge.

The only dramatic parts of Chiuma's trial were the closing statements, which referred in one way or another to the trials of Ohsugi and Taniguchi and the results of those trials.

The defense pointed out that Chiuma had been a witness for the prosecution in the Taniguchi trial, and thus he had aided the U.S. government and had been "truthful and forthright" in doing so. (Chiuma, of course, had not been completely "truthful and forthright"; he had lied about who was in charge of the executions.)

The defense then pointed out that both Ohsugi, who gave the execution order, and Taniguchi, who saw that it was carried out, received life sentences, and the others involved received ten years each. The attorney asked that his client receive similar treatment in sentencing as had the others. This request revealed why Taniguchi's original death sentence had been reduced to life in prison and his co-defendants' life sentences had been reduced to ten years. All convictions in the war crimes trials automatically went before a War Crimes Commission review board. The board members who reviewed the Taniguchi trial thought Taniguchi's death sentence was too harsh in view of the fact that Ohsugi, who was the most culpable of those involved, received only a life sentence. Therefore, they reduced Taniguchi's sentence to life in prison and the life sentences of the others to ten years each.

The defense counsel for Chiuma concluded with a statement about why Chiuma was pleading guilty to killing Goodwin.

> I would like to state this, that this accused has volun-
> tarily pleaded guilty. He was not talked into it or advised
> about it. His comrades with whom he participated in this
> perpetration have been sentenced and he too desires to
> be sentenced. . . .
>
> I submit that in pleading guilty to Specification 1
> [the killing of Lieutenant Goodwin], except to the words
> "wrongfully and unlawfully," this accused committed
> this act under orders and at that time the execution of
> such orders was not wrongful and unlawful. However,
> they were violations of the Laws and Customs of
> War, and so the accused has pleaded guilty, since the
> original order has been found to be an illegal order and
> men of superior rank and position were sentenced.

The prosecutor, in his closing statement, asserted that Chiuma deserved the death penalty even though no other defendant was to be executed for the Kendari killings. The prosecutor made his case by referring to the report of the board that had reviewed the results of Ohsugi's trial.

> The review authority made a very interesting state-
> ment in looking over Ohsugi's case, and I will just read
> it: "The accused stands guilty of murder of these men.
> The details are shown in the foregoing review. He has
> been shown justice [life in prison instead of death]. He
> is probably a very bewildered Japanese and has pon-
> dered, no doubt, why he has been shown such justice.
> Why the decision was not made to execute him is not

within the providence of this review. He is a very lucky Japanese in not having received the death sentence. This expresses the opinion of this reviewer. Ohsugi had a fair trial and the sentence of life imprisonment that was handed down was certainly not prejudicial to him—only prejudicial to the memory of the thirteen airmen who did not deserve to die.

Then the Taniguchi Review Authority accepts that mistake [by reducing Taniguchi's death sentence to life imprisonment], and it is our contention that mistake had been followed right on down. I think this Commission should consider the evidence in this case in determining its decision, and determine the decision actually from the evidence before it and not feel that it is bound hard and fast by former review opinions. That is all.

The prosecution's effort to convince the court to consider a death sentence was unsuccessful. Chiuma was found guilty on both charges and was sentenced to ten years in prison.

So ended the trials in which most of the Japanese responsible for the deaths of the nine PBY crewmen were brought to justice. A few of those involved never stood before the War Crimes Commission. In the 103rd Antiaircraft Unit, Lieutenant (jg) Nakata selected Otani, a chief petty officer, to behead one of the Americans (Edwin McMaster, Walter Price, or Henry Zollinger) at the airfield. Otani escaped prosecution because he was killed in an Allied bombing raid a few weeks after the Kendari executions. Chief Warrant Officer Abe, the senior noncommissioned officer of the Tokkei Tai, committed suicide after the war to avoid being charged with war crimes. The aircraft maintenance unit commanded by Captain Moritama killed one of the three Americans at the airfield, but the actual executioner was never identified. From the maintenance unit only Moritama was tried and convicted.

Another person who escaped the court was the man who beheaded Joe Sommer; he too was never identified. This individual escaped trial because the American authorities believed Katsuhito Imai and Toshisuke Tanabe when they claimed that Sommer had been shot by a firing squad, not beheaded. It might very well have been Imai who hacked Joe Sommer to death.

Also escaping trial was the officer who arranged the executions of Sommer, McMaster, Price, and Zollinger. Someone coordinated the complex arrangements of transporting the prisoners from Kendari, setting the times of the executions, working with the different military units, and digging the graves. This person was never identified and brought to justice.

Chapter 14

The American Families

Almost four years after the eleven American airmen of PBY No. 08233 were killed, the sentencing of Sazae Chiuma brought the war trials to an end. But unfortunately, the tragedy was not over for the crewmen's families.

The families of the dead crewmen knew nothing about the war crimes investigations. Except for official notification from the Navy Department that their loved ones were missing in action, the families learned very little from the U.S. government about the fate of their boys. The Navy sent only one other official notice— a heart-wrenching letter telling that the airmen's status was changed to killed in action, effective one year from the date they had been reported missing.

From the day the war ended in the Pacific, the families of the missing men hoped and prayed that their boys would turn up in one of the Japanese prisoner-of-war camps or would be found hiding on some small island. As the weeks and months passed, their hopes faded.

The families were not idle during this time. In early 1945, long before the war ended, they started to contact each other for comfort and to share meager bits of information. Without knowing it, they formed what today would be called a mutual support group.

Through letters, photographs, phone calls, and visits, most of the relatives became acquainted with one another. The only families not involved were those of Walter Price and Joe Sommer. All letters sent to the Price family were returned unopened; Joe Sommer's parents were not alive, and no relative communicated with the other families.

Lieutenant Goodwin was the only one of the eleven airmen who had married. His wife, Valerie, wrote letters from Australia and visited some of the families when she came to the United States to introduce her little son, Michael, to his American grandparents. Michael, who had been born some months after his father's death, was the only offspring of any of the airmen.

Although the families kept in close contact, they searched for information in separate ways. William F. Goodwin, Sr., sought the help of his friend U.S. Sen. David I. Walsh, chairman of the Senate Committee on Naval Affairs, in the hopes that Walsh could cut through the red tape and find out what happened to Lieutenant Goodwin. But even Senator Walsh could not discover any additional information.

Several weeks after Lieutenant Goodwin was reported missing, his parents received letters from some of his former squadron mates. The Goodwins wrote to each of them repeatedly, pumping them for any scrap of information, but their son's friends could not add much to what the Goodwins already knew. And because of security regulations, the men could not even tell the parents where their son's PBY was going the night it was shot down.

The Goodwins eventually learned about Kendari and its location from Helen Schenck, the mother of pilot Jack Schenck. Her husband, William, also a Navy officer, asked friends and acquaintances in the Pentagon for information, and they told him that his son's PBY had crashed near Kendari in the Celebes Islands. This information quickly spread through the group of families. Helen Schenck later haunted the halls of the Department of the Navy in Washington, D.C., in her search for further information.

Jake Nilva's older brother, Allen, was highly placed in the U.S. military's Far East Legal Section, and he made inquiries through this channel. He wrote home to report that six of the crew members were found buried near where the plane went down and that his brother was not among them. This news was wrong, of course, and from the false information, Allen Nilva wrongly deduced that the remaining five, including his brother, were still alive.

Bessie (Nilva) Frisch, one of Jake's sisters, corresponded with Jake's shipmates. She took over the task of corresponding for the Nilva family because her parents were old and deeply upset about Jake's disappearance. Jake's shipmates could offer very little information, and some of what they passed on, with the best of intentions, turned out to be false. One of Jake's friends said Nilva's last mission was in the southern Philippines, more than a thousand miles from where the PBY actually crashed. Some families heard incorrectly that the Japanese had shot all the plane's crew members.

As the months dragged by, the truth of what had happened remained hidden from the families. The desperate searches for information went on at the same time the war crimes investigations were under way, the bodies were recovered and identified, and the trials were conducted. Still the government failed to tell the families anything factual.

The families would finally learn the true story from an unexpected source: the newspapers. On February 27, 1947, nearly all the families learned the horrifying story of their sons' beheadings either from reading it in their local newspapers or from reporters who telephoned to ask for an interview.

Without first informing the families, the U.S. military authorities in occupied Japan had issued a statement to the press on the trials of the Japanese involved in the Kendari killings. The Associated Press put out a news article that named the nine men who had been executed and listed their hometowns.

Bill and Catherine Goodwin learned of the ultimate fate of their son from a *Boston Globe* reporter who called before running the story in his paper. The reporter was stunned to discover that the families had not been informed before the story was released to the press.

New waves of shock and grief swept through the families. The Goodwins quickly cabled their daughter-in-law in Australia, and Valerie Goodwin received the shocking news a few days later, after returning from a short holiday. Valerie Goodwin's son was only two years old and did not understand what all the commotion was about.

Even after repeated calls and questions from the families, the Navy Department in Washington, D.C., would not confirm or deny the story. Official notification of the finding of the remains of six of the fliers did not reach the families until March 11, 1947—two weeks after the news story had hit the papers. This official Navy Department letter provided even less information than the press releases.

As it did to all the families involved, the U.S. Navy sent yet another letter to Bill Goodwin's parents. Dated March 26, 1947, the one-paragraph missive said only that Goodwin had been shot down, captured, and killed. It mentioned that four other crew members were killed with him but did not give their names.

Now the families of the nine who had been executed knew the truth, but not the details, of their sons' fate. The Schencks and the Kuhlmans, however, were still without any official news of their sons, Lt. Jack Schenck and Ensign Arthur Kuhlman. The news stories and the official letters mentioned only the nine executed crewmen, and said nothing about Schenck or Kuhlman. The Kuhlmans held a slim hope their son was still alive, but the Schencks believed that theirs was dead. It was many more months before the Navy officially notified the Schencks and the Kuhlmans that their sons had been killed in the crash of the PBY.

Shortly after the Goodwins learned of their son's execution, they received a visit from his high-school buddy Tommy Ruggeiro. Ruggeiro told them that he had known for a couple of months that his closest friend had been killed, and even how he had died. He had learned about it from Helen Schenck, with whom he had been corresponding as part of his own search for information.

Helen Schenck had visited the Navy Department in Washington, D.C., several months earlier and had learned the story from

someone in the Navy. Her contact told her that a PBY had been
shot down about the same time her son's PBY was reported missing,
and that the crew had either been killed outright or executed soon
afterward. This was still unofficial news, and the identification of
the crew was not positively known. Mrs. Schenck kept the information from the members of the other families except Allen Nilva
and Bessie Frisch, Jake Nilva's brother and sister. On November
27, 1946, she wrote to Allen Nilva with the story that, while incor-
rect in certain details, seemed to confirm the tragic news:

> Dear Allen,
>   Once again my "hunch" was correct! There was news
> awaiting me at Bu. of Pers. It is our plane, Allen. So the
> long wait of 2 years & nearly two mos. is at an end. In a
> week or a month the other ten parents will be notified
> as I was, on Oct. 10th. Please tell Bess now. I can't bear
> to write it. Words look even more terrible. Tell her how
> I longed to tell them, but did keep my promise to
> Wash. D.C. to "Tell no Parents". Any day now, Bess (if
> home instead of Fla.) will receive and read those horri-
> ble words "Jake executed". The shock will be so awful,
> so now is the time to tell her. Your dear mother must
> never know.
>   The cable read, Japs finally admitted that Pilot and
> one of other officer died in the crash landing of the dis-
> abled plane. Other officer and three of crew executed &
> buried near plane (that accounts for the six graves, Allen,
> mentioned in the first cable). The four other crewmen
> taken to an airfield (Jap) 30 miles away and executed—
> each by a different group. Oh God! It is so terrible. I
> wish they had all died in landing. I'm in bed, under a
> doctors care, so all for now. Please write.
>   Helen Schenck

    Helen Schenck told Tommy Ruggeiro the sad news only after
he promised not to tell Bill and Catherine Goodwin. There was a

slim chance that the downed plane was not the one commanded by her son. But when official word was finally received about Lieutenant Goodwin's death, Tommy visited the Goodwins' to tell them what he knew.

Tommy would remain close to his best friend's parents for the rest of their lives, and he remains close to his friend's widow to this day. From the time he returned home from the war in Europe until Catherine Goodwin passed away, Ruggeiro sent flowers to her every Mother's Day as a tribute to his lost friend.

In March 1947 Allen Nilva finally was able to contact a person who could pass on vital information about what happened to his brother Jake. This was Thomas J. O'Connor, chief prosecutor in the Taniguchi trial. After learning O'Connor's name from an Associated Press story, Allen Nilva wrote to him in care of the War Crimes Commission, explaining the families' frustration and asking for information.

O'Connor sent back an eleven-page letter telling Nilva everything he could about the Taniguchi trial. In divulging this information, O'Connor actually broke government regulations. Knowing from Allen Nilva's letter that Nilva was an attorney, O'Connor briefly explained how the war crimes trial machinery was set up and how the prosecutors and defense attorneys were recruited. And he pointed out his low opinion of defense counsel in the Taniguchi trial, writing, "The defense summation, I hate to think of it, the case was a tissue of lies, made out of the whole cloth."

O'Connor's letter went on to tell of his investigative trip to Kendari and the results of the trial. He concluded with a list of some final points:

1. All the boys arrived in Kendari on Oct. 6, 1944.
2. They were questioned for about a week, then kept there until November 25th, 1944.
3. They were executed on November 25th, 1944, between 4:30 P.M. and 5:00 P.M. in the afternoon—no trial, no court-martial.
4. From my own personal investigation and after

interviewing many witnesses I know they were not mistreated nor tortured during the period.

     5. From all reports, Japanese and natives, they died smiling like the gallant men they were.

     6. I don't know whether Jake Nilva was short or tall, but talking to Japanese prisoners I learned even before I had seen the list of the crew members that there was a little Jewish lad among the Americans, and all of the crew seemed to like him.

O'Connor's final remarks were not entirely correct. The nine survivors reached Kendari on October 8, not October 6. They were questioned almost continually for two weeks, not one week. The accepted date for the execution of the group of five men that included Nilva is November 24, not November 25.

O'Connor's statement that the men were not tortured or mistreated is the strangest of his errors. A great deal of circumstantial evidence shows that they were at least beaten, if not tortured. O'Connor may have lied about this to spare Jake's parents further grief. But it is curious that someone so close to the case, who had access to all the evidence and had visited the scene, could get so many of the basic facts wrong.

Chapter 15

Coming Home

In March 1947 a joint American and Australian Graves Registration recovery team found the remains of five men in the common grave behind the Tokkei Tai prison compound in Kendari. All that remained were skeletons and a few pieces of tattered clothing. Each skeleton's head had been severed from its body.

The Graves Registration team tagged the five skeletons, placed them in coffins, and flew them to Makassar, regional capital of the Celebes. There the coffins joined the remains of other war dead. Then they were flown to Barrackpore, India, a main identification center for the remains of American service personnel killed in the Pacific war.

The identification of the five bodies from Kendari was made relatively easy because of a scrap of U.S. Navy–issue clothing found in the grave. Stenciled on the piece of uniform was the name Raymond L. Cart. Graves Registration learned from an inquiry to Washington, D.C., that Raymond Lawrence Cart, from Paris Crossing, Indiana, had been an aviation machinist mate 3rd class on a Navy PBY Catalina patrol plane commanded by Lt. Jack Schenck—a plane that had failed to return to its base after a mission on the night of October 1, 1944.

Navy personnel sent the military dental records of the men

on that plane to Barrackpore. With the help of the dental charts, the bodies of four of the men were positively identified as Cart, Bill Goodwin, Jake Nilva, and Harvey Harbecke in February 1947.

The remains of the fifth victim could not be positively identified and were tagged "Unknown X-203." Good dental records for Paul Schilling were not available, but the dental work of X-203 did not match any of the other men still unaccounted for, and further investigation proved that the remains marked as X-203 were those of Paul Schilling. Five of the eleven crew members of the downed PBY patrol plane had now been identified.

The search for the remains of the other six crew members continued in Kendari. With the help of local Indonesians, the Graves Registration team found another grave some ten miles from Kendari. In it was a single skeleton, the head cut from its body. A Royal Australian Army dentist, Captain Ian S. Noble, performed a brief field examination. He judged that the skeleton was that of a white male, probably an American or Australian because of the good quality of the dental work. These remains were also flown to Barrackpore, where dental comparison confirmed the identity of another missing crewman, Joe Sommer.

Though the search went on, the remains of the last five crew members were not found. The common grave of Edwin McMaster, Walter G. Price, and Henry T. Zollinger, thought to be near the Japanese airfield, was never located. Apparently there was little effort to find the remains of Jack Schenck and Arthur Kuhlman, the two men who died during the October 1944 PBY mission. Eventually the military classified the bodies of these five men as unrecoverable, and they gave up the search.

The six bodies that had been identified were buried in a temporary military cemetery in Barrackpore. Toward the end of 1947, the Department of the Navy sent a letter to Bill Goodwin's widow asking where she wanted her husband to be permanently buried. National cemeteries were being prepared nationwide to receive America's war dead, and this letter, and similar letters sent to each of the families, suggested that one of these new cemeteries might be an appropriate burial place. Nevertheless, the Navy left the decision to each family.

By this time Valerie Goodwin had met another young man and was getting ready to marry again. She thought it best that Bill Goodwin's parents be the ones to select the final resting place for their only son, and she forwarded the necessary papers on to them. After much thought the Goodwins selected the then-uncompleted National Cemetery of the Pacific in Hawaii. Before he left for the war their son had told them that if he was killed, he wanted to be buried with his comrades. Interment in a national cemetery would fulfill that wish. And since Goodwin's widow and his son were living in Australia and his parents were in Plymouth, Massachusetts, a resting place in Hawaii—halfway between those he loved the most—seemed the most logical.

On March 11, 1949, William F. Goodwin, Jr., was buried in grave F-586 in the National Cemetery of the Pacific, Honolulu, Hawaii, with full military honors. It was his birthday; he would have been twenty-nine.

The National Cemetery of the Pacific is situated in an ancient volcanic crater, commonly known as the "Punchbowl" because of its shape. The site is just behind the city, only about a mile from Waikiki Beach. To the ancient Hawaiians, it was the Hill of Sacrifice, where those who broke the laws of the islands were ceremoniously put to death and their bodies were burned on an altar of stone at the highest point on the crater rim. The islanders consider this crater a sacred and solemn place, a fitting site for a national cemetery.

It is, perhaps, the most beautiful of all of America's national cemeteries. The extinct volcanic crater that holds Bill Goodwin and thousands of other Americans who gave their lives for their country is an almost perfectly shaped bowl that rises hundreds of feet above the surrounding land. The cemetery has no traditional upright headstones; each engraved stone marker lies flush with the manicured lawn. Beautiful tropical trees are placed sparingly around the grounds.

The first interments at the new cemetery took place in January 1949, when almost 12,000 of the dead from World War II were buried with proper ceremony, but the cemetery did not open to the public until July 19, 1949. Bill Goodwin's parents visited their son's grave only once, in the early 1950s.

Although Goodwin was buried thousands of miles from Plymouth, his parents and hometown did not fail to honor his memory. The Goodwins placed a memorial plaque in their family cemetery plot. The town placed his name on a memorial in front of Veterans Hall, which honors those from Plymouth who died in World War II, and named a road after him. Goodwin Road, near the summer home of the Goodwin family, was originally cut through the woods by hand by Bill Goodwin, Jr., and his father in the late 1930s.

The five other crewmen whose remains had been identified were sent home for burial, as their families requested. Harvey Harbecke was buried in his hometown of Fowler, Colorado, in May 1948. Jake Nilva was buried in the Sons of Jacob Cemetery in St. Paul, Minnesota. Raymond Cart was buried in the Coffee Creek Cemetery in Paris Crossing, Indiana. Joe Sommer was buried in the new Beverly National Cemetery, at Beverly, New Jersey. The last to be brought home was Paul Schilling, who was laid to rest in June 1949 in St. Mary's Cemetery, at Clinton, New York.

Although the remains of the other five crewmen were never found, the men were not forgotten. The names of Edwin McMaster, Walter Price, and Henry Zollinger are inscribed on the walls of the Courts of the Missing at the National Cemetery of the Pacific, just a few hundred feet from Bill Goodwin's grave. The names of Jack Schenck and Arthur Kuhlman are inscribed on the rectangular piers of the hemicycles surrounding the memorial chapel at the Manila American Cemetery, in the Philippines.

It is possible that the remains of these five men may still be recovered. The evidence indicates that Graves Registration was wrong in assuming that the remains of McMaster, Price, and Zollinger could not be found. The Indonesian worker Johan Tomasawa knew where the grave was, as he told war crimes investigators in April

1947. He said that the grave was not destroyed by Allied bombing and that he marked the grave at the end of the war. But Graves Registration never received this information.

Although Tomasawa has probably long since died, the site of this grave should not be too difficult to find. The small villages on the road between Kendari and the airfield would have been near the execution site. Natives in the area who still remember the incident could probably locate the grave site.

The remains of pilots Schenck and Kuhlman might still be found as well. The nine survivors of the PBY crash carried their bodies ashore and buried them not far from the village of Paku on the small island of Bungkinkela, so the grave's general site is known.

It is not too late to reopen efforts to recover the remains of the missing five men. Only then will the tragic story of these eleven young sailors be truly brought to an end.

Epilogue

In 1948, long after learning the truth about how her brother Jake died at the hands of the Japanese, Bessie Frisch read an article in *Newsweek* magazine about war criminals executed by the Allies. The article mentioned that the widow of Tojo, prime minister of Japan during the war, wanted the United States to return her husband's body to her "in the name of humanity." Angered at that phrase, Bessie wrote in a letter to the magazine: "To my brother, Jake Henry Nilva, and his buddies: We have not forgotten and we pray to God for guidance to those in whose hands lies the power of justice to your aggressors."

She included a photo of Jake in which he is sitting on the steps of the war memorial atop a hill in Kings Park, overlooking Perth in Australia. A plaque on the memorial reads "Lest We Forget." *Newsweek* printed the letter and photo in its January 3, 1949, issue. The memorial in the photo was also the favorite spot of young Valerie Storey and Bill Goodwin—my parents—when they were getting to know each other.

Although Bessie Frisch did not realize it when she wrote to *Newsweek*, the Japanese responsible for the deaths of her brother and the other eight American airmen had been found guilty and sent to prison. Convicted Japanese war criminals from all across the Pacific served their sentences in Tokyo's Sagumo prison, which was run by General MacArthur's command in occupied Japan.

Bessie Frisch also did not know that, although many Japanese war criminals came to trial and were convicted, the justice she desired was not to be. The Japanese guilty of thousands of brutal war crimes would not have to serve much of their prison terms. Within months of the trials' completion, the system that sentenced the criminals to prison started to set them free. Some were paroled; others were given clemency and released outright. By 1956 the Sagumo prison population was reduced to 383 from an original total of about 2,000. Within two more years, all the prisoners had been released, and Sagumo prison was closed down.

The maximum prison time that anyone served, no matter how heinous the crime, was thirteen years. Unless the families of the nine Americans murdered at Kendari happened to read a brief article in the *New York Times* toward the end of 1958, they never realized that the killers of their sons had been released by the victims' own government. Very few people in the United States, including those who had suffered under their cruel hand, realized how lightly the guilty Japanese were punished. Some spent less time in confinement than many of the prisoners they had held under their brutal control during the war years.

In Europe, war criminals from Nazi Germany were also tried before military tribunals. As in Japan, the wartime leaders were brought together in one big, well-publicized trial. Most were convicted, and some went to the gallows while others received prison sentences ranging from ten years to life. Thousands of less-publicized war criminals were tried, and most of them were sent to prison. As in Japan, many were released early.

At first glance it might seem that Japanese and German war criminals were treated much the same. But in reality the Japanese fared much better. Though all Japanese war criminals were released by 1958, the Allies in Germany were determined to keep at least a few of their convicts in Spandau prison. Some served out their full terms and were eventually released; others died of old age in prison.

The last Spandau inmate died in the prison in 1987, forty-two years after the war had ended.

Further, an active worldwide effort to track down suspected Nazi war criminals is still underway. In addition to searches by the United States, Israel, and Germany, the World War II Allies still have both government and private groups investigating. As recently as December 1993, a former German officer was put on trial in Germany for killing Italian civilians fifty years earlier. Israel has tried two suspected Nazi war criminals: Adolf Eichmann in the 1960s and John Demjanjuk in the 1980s. Eichmann was convicted and executed; Demjanjuk finally was released by the Israeli courts as not guilty.

No such searches have been organized for Japanese war criminals. After the war crimes trials of the late 1940s, investigations into the World War II conduct of the Japanese simply came to a halt. No one continued the search for any Japanese who might have escaped prosecution. One might think, erroneously, that all surviving Japanese who committed war atrocities had been found and tried.

The families of my father and of the other ten airmen who went down with him could find no organizations to press for information about personnel missing in action, like those that later developed out of the Vietnam War. All the parents of the eleven men passed away never fully knowing what had happened to their loved ones. Sara Nilva, Jake Nilva's mother, died still believing her son would come home one day. All the correct information existed, but it had not been brought together or released. It is shameful that the parents of these men never learned the answers to their questions.

While piecing together my research, I thought the handling of the Kendari war crimes trials was strange. Since General MacArthur exerted a great deal of pressure to conduct the trials quickly, why were there four separate trials instead of only one, or perhaps two? Admiral Ohsugi may have needed a separate trial because of the unrelated executions in Makassar, but all the other accused men

from the Kendari area should have been tried together. The same
witnesses, evidence, and written statements were relevant to all
the trials.

Because there were four trials—each with different judges,
prosecutors, and defense attorneys—many of the common threads
were lost. Facts discussed in one trial were overlooked or ignored
in another. Johan Tomasawa, a key witness in the Furukawa trial,
spent little time on the stand in the Taniguchi trial. He would have
been a good witness in both trials.

Another problem was the lack of cooperation between the War
Crimes Commission and Graves Registration. The prosecution in
the Furukawa trial commented in court that Graves Registration
had withheld information that could have been used in the earlier
trials. The medical and dental reports on the remains of Joe
Sommer are prime examples: Though written in October 1946,
the reports were not made available to the War Crimes Commission until the Chiuma trial in 1948.

The grave of Edwin McMaster, Walter Price, and Henry
Zollinger might have been found if information had been flowing
in the other direction as well. Witnesses to the executions and
information on the grave's location were available, but the War
Crimes Commission never passed the word along to Graves
Registration. But the men's remains might yet be brought home.
My research has tentatively located the general site of this grave,
and witnesses to the execution of the three men are still alive as of
this writing.

The actual location of the airplane crash site and the remains
of pilots Jack Schenck and Art Kuhlman were not readily apparent
in the documentation originating from the late 1940s. All the
papers I looked at said my father's plane crashed just off Salabangka Island. Although there is a small island with that name, it
is part of a dozen or so small islands known collectively as the
Salabangka Islands.

It was not until 1989 that I learned of the island of Bungkinkela
and of the island village of Paku, near which the plane sank. I got
this information from a Dutch freelance writer, Michiel Hegener,

who had stumbled across a reference to the capture of my father's crew while researching a book he was writing on Dutch guerrilla warfare against the Japanese in the Salabangka area. Had the war crimes investigators or Graves Registration done a little more work, they could have located the grave site and recovered the remains of Schenck and Kuhlman. The plane is still there, and my research shows that the remains of Schenck and Kuhlman are buried on Bungkinkela. It is still possible that they could be found.

My final thoughts are of the Japanese themselves. The Japanese culture seems to have changed a great deal since World War II. In the 1930s and 1940s, the Japanese nation acted as though it had a right to take whatever it wanted and to treat all non-Japanese as it saw fit. From those in positions of power to the lowest ranks of the population, both civilian and military, the Japanese believed their destiny was to rule Asia.

The high-ranking officers involved with the Kendari murders— Ohsugi, Furukawa, Sonokawa, and Taniguchi—were highly educated, articulate, mature, and experienced men. Most were graduates of Japan's Naval Academy, the equivalent of our U.S. Naval Academy, and yet these men acted no better than lowly, uneducated Japanese enlisted soldiers or seamen fresh from a farm. In the Japanese military, brutality was normal and accepted behavior.

The higher in rank the accused war criminals were, the louder they cried their innocence. Some of the ensigns and lieutenants were willing to admit their guilt, at least during the war crimes investigations. Others simply kept quiet and let the court decide their fate. The captains and admirals, however, either claimed ignorance of what was happening under their direct command or gave the court long, complicated stories of why they were not guilty of the murders they were so deeply involved in.

I cannot say that I hate the Japanese people of today for the executions of my father and the other airmen more than fifty years ago, in November 1944. Most, if not all, of those directly involved have died. Very few of the Japanese who fought in the

Pacific during World War II are involved today in their government or industry. One cannot blame the children or grandchildren for the crimes of those who came before them. In Germany today, however, the people at least admit to their nation's crimes and atrocities. Japan still does not. The Japanese generally ignore what their nation did throughout the Pacific region fifty years ago.

Only recently has the government of Japan started to talk openly about the country's behavior in the war, and not without controversy. In August 1993, Morihiro Hosokawa took office as prime minister, and one of his first acts was to publicly express "profound remorse and apologies for the fact that Japan's actions, including acts of aggression and colonial rule, caused unbearable suffering and sorrow for so many people." This open apology sparked harsh responses from other high government officials. Some members of Japan's House of Representatives called Hosokawa's apology a blasphemy against history and demanded that he retract the statement. One member of the House, Shintaro Ishihara, went so far as to say, "Those indiscreet remarks without solid historical viewpoints deserve death." Many people in Japan still refuse to face the truth or, even worse, think Japan did nothing wrong during the war.

The people of Japan would find that they would get along much better with the rest of the world if they would face the fact that they and their leadership were the source of a great deal of suffering during the first half of this century.

Bibliography

UNPUBLISHED SOURCES

Flight log books of Gardner Burt (from Gardner Burt); Raymond L. Cart (from the Cart family); George Castille (from George J. Castille); George Favorite (from George U. Favorite); William F. Goodwin, Jr. (from the author's collection); Lauren E. Johnson (from L. E. "Steve" Johnson); Arthur W. Kuhlman (from the Kuhlman family); William Martin (from William H. Martin); Jake H. Nilva (from the Nilva family); and H. V. Smith (from H. V. "Bud" Smith).

Reviews of the Yokohama Class B and Class C War Crimes Trials. Record Group 331. National Archives.

USS *Tangier* Deck Log. U.S. Navy Historical Center, Navy Yard, Washington, D.C.

VP-101 War Diary. U.S. Navy Historical Center, Navy Yard, Washington, D.C.

VP-33 War Diary. U.S. Navy Historical Center, Navy Yard, Washington, D.C.

War Crimes Trial Record, *"The United States v. Gosuke Taniguchi et al."* Record Group 331, Case #307. National Archives.

War Crimes Trial Record, *"The United States v. Marikazu Ohsugi."* Record Group 153. National Archives.

War Crimes Trial Record, *"The United States* v. *Sazae Chiuma."* Record Group 331, Cases #307 & 336. National Archives.
War Crimes Trial Record, *"The United States* v. *Tamotsu Furukawa* et al." Record Group 331, Case #307. National Archives.

BOOKS

Creed, Roscoe. *PBY: The Catalina Flying Boat.* Annapolis, MD: Naval Institute Press, 1985.
Hayes, Robert W. *Bless 'Em All.* Eden Prairie, MN: Willow Creek Publishers, 1986.
Kerr, E. Bartlett. *Surrender & Survival.* New York: William Morrow and Company, 1985.
Mueller, A. J. *Black Cats with Wings of Gold.* Haverford, PA: VPB-33 Reunion Group, 1992.

Index